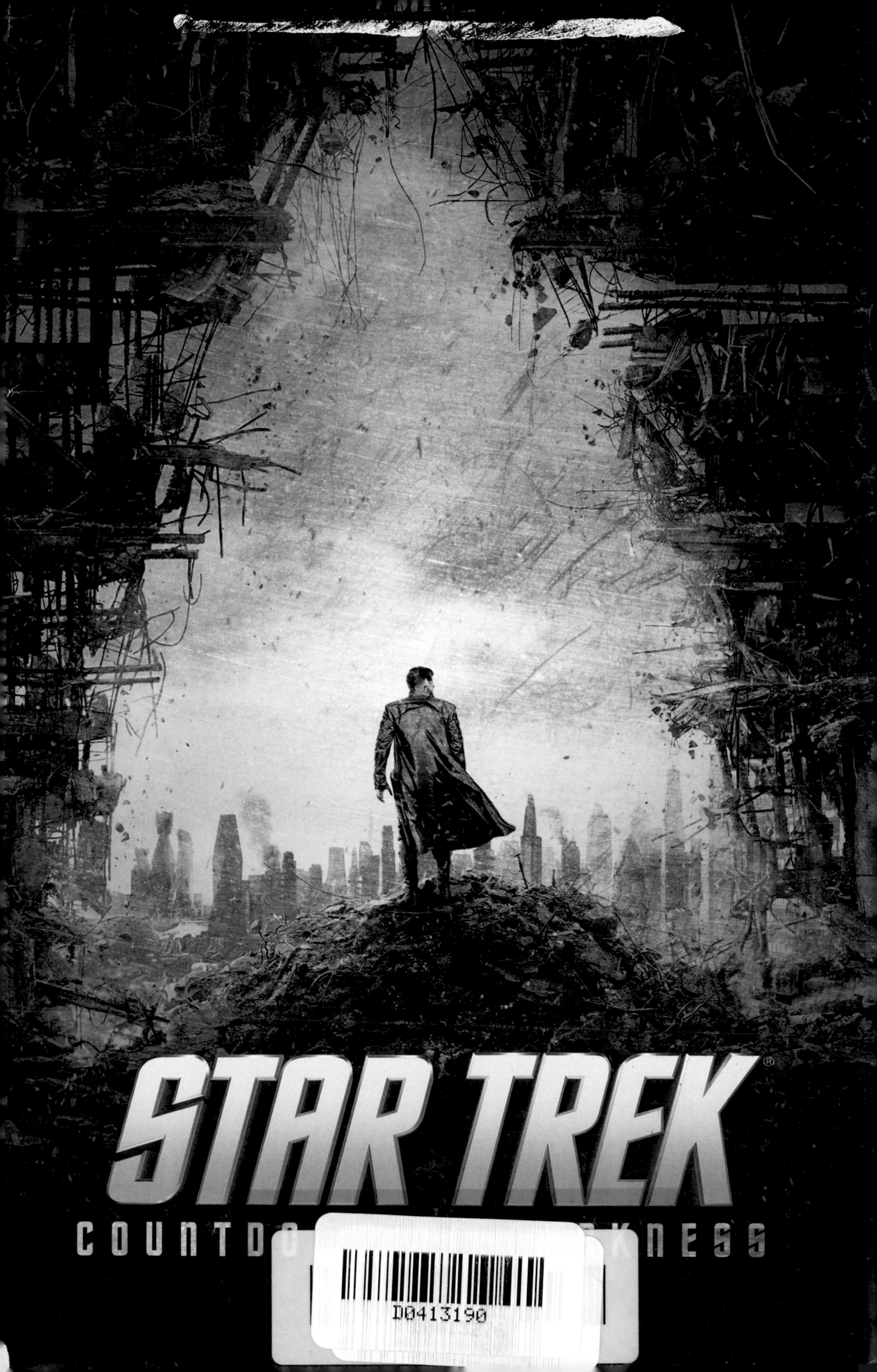

STAR TREK®

COUNTDO[illegible]KNESS

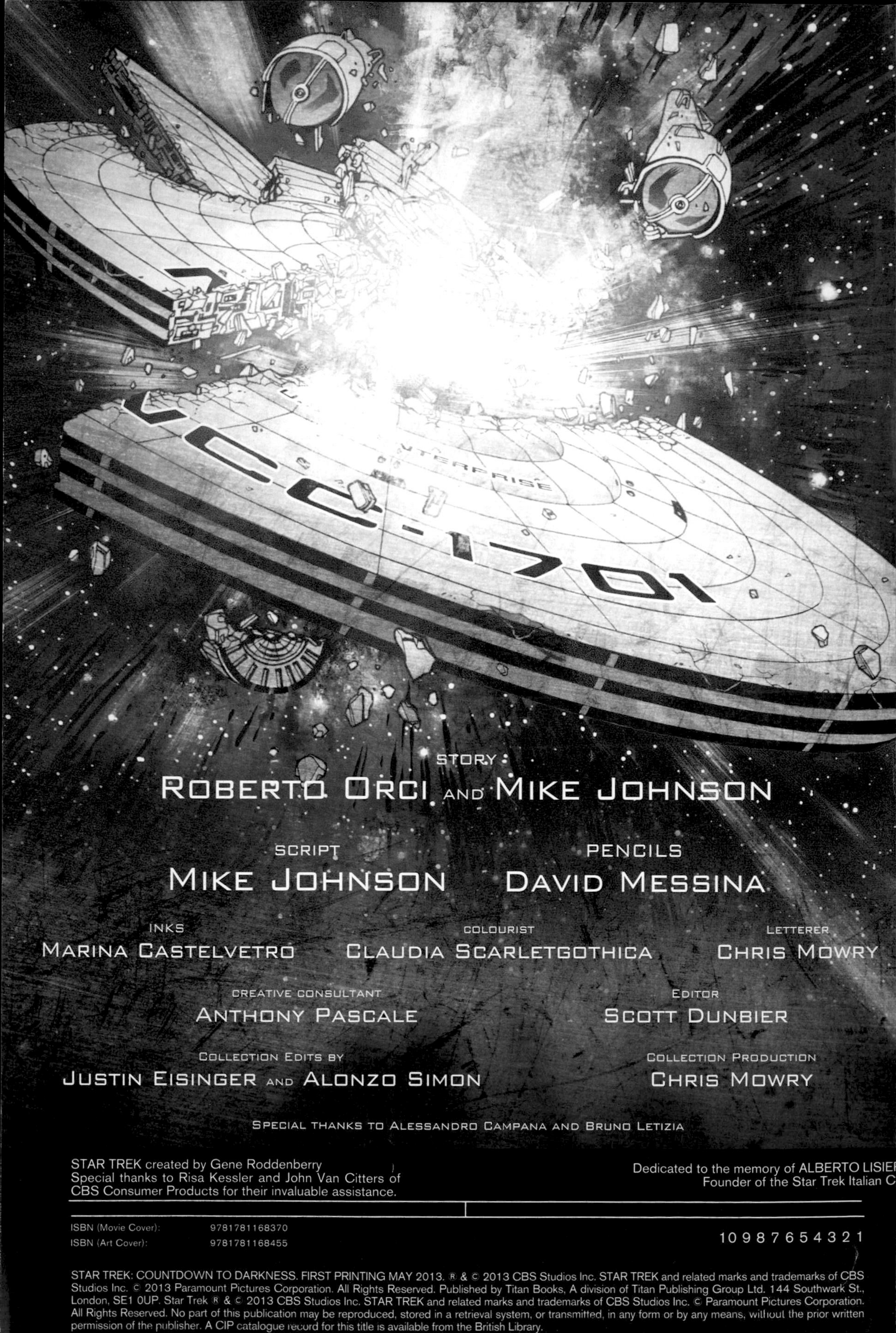

NTERPRISE
CC-1701

STORY
ROBERTO ORCI AND MIKE JOHNSON

SCRIPT
MIKE JOHNSON

PENCILS
DAVID MESSINA

INKS
MARINA CASTELVETRO

COLOURIST
CLAUDIA SCARLETGOTHICA

LETTERER
CHRIS MOWRY

CREATIVE CONSULTANT
ANTHONY PASCALE

EDITOR
SCOTT DUNBIER

COLLECTION EDITS BY
JUSTIN EISINGER AND ALONZO SIMON

COLLECTION PRODUCTION
CHRIS MOWRY

SPECIAL THANKS TO ALESSANDRO CAMPANA AND BRUNO LETIZIA

STAR TREK created by Gene Roddenberry
Special thanks to Risa Kessler and John Van Citters of CBS Consumer Products for their invaluable assistance.

Dedicated to the memory of ALBERTO LISIEI
Founder of the Star Trek Italian C

ISBN (Movie Cover): 9781781168370
ISBN (Art Cover): 9781781168455

10 9 8 7 6 5 4 3 2 1

STAR TREK: COUNTDOWN TO DARKNESS. FIRST PRINTING MAY 2013. Published by Titan Books, A division of Titan Publishing Group Ltd. 144 Southwark St., London, SE1 0UP. A CIP catalogue record for this title is available from the British Library.

Art by David Messina
Colours by Claudia Scarletgothica

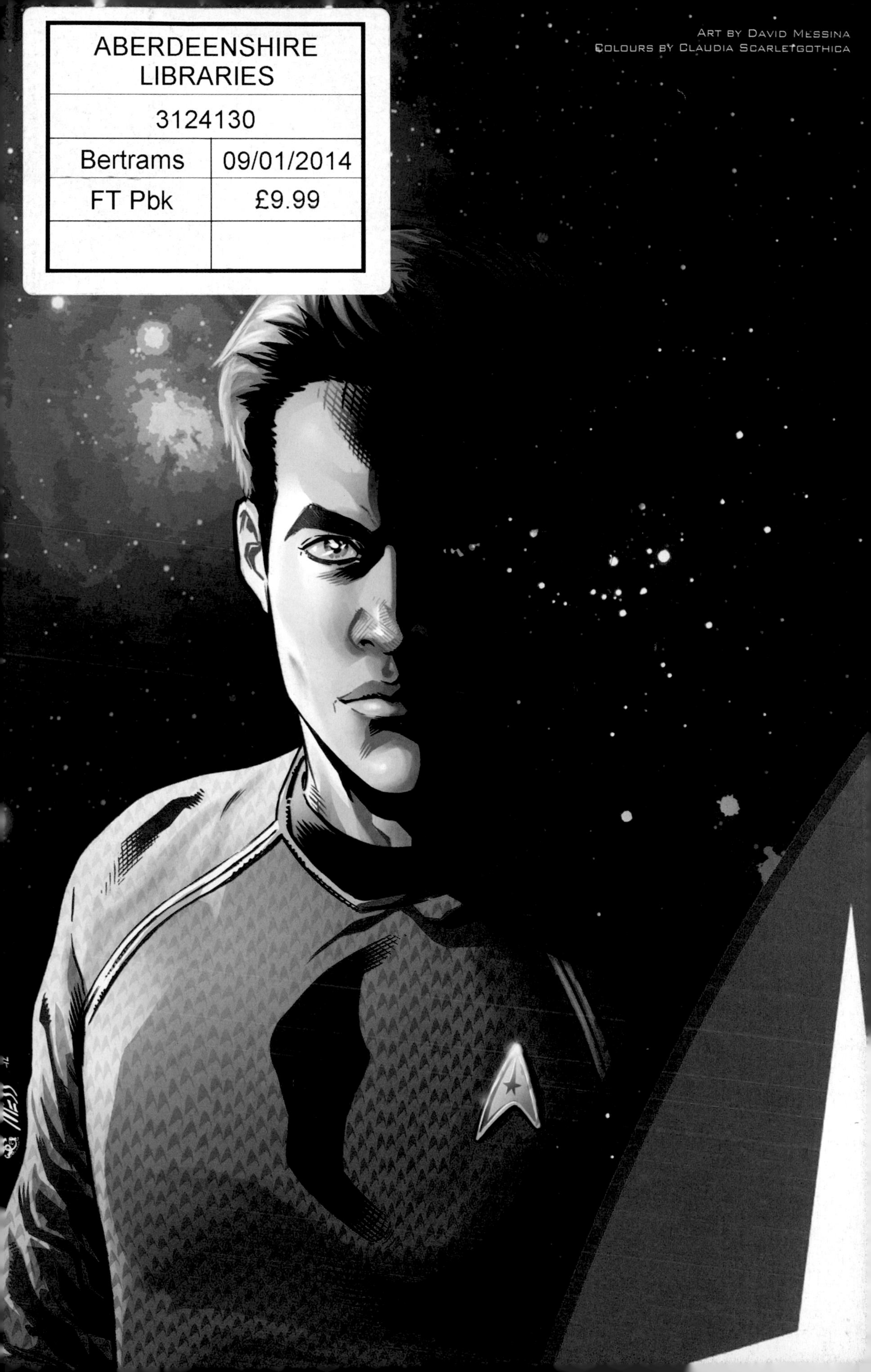

Art by Stephen Molnar
Colours by John Rauch

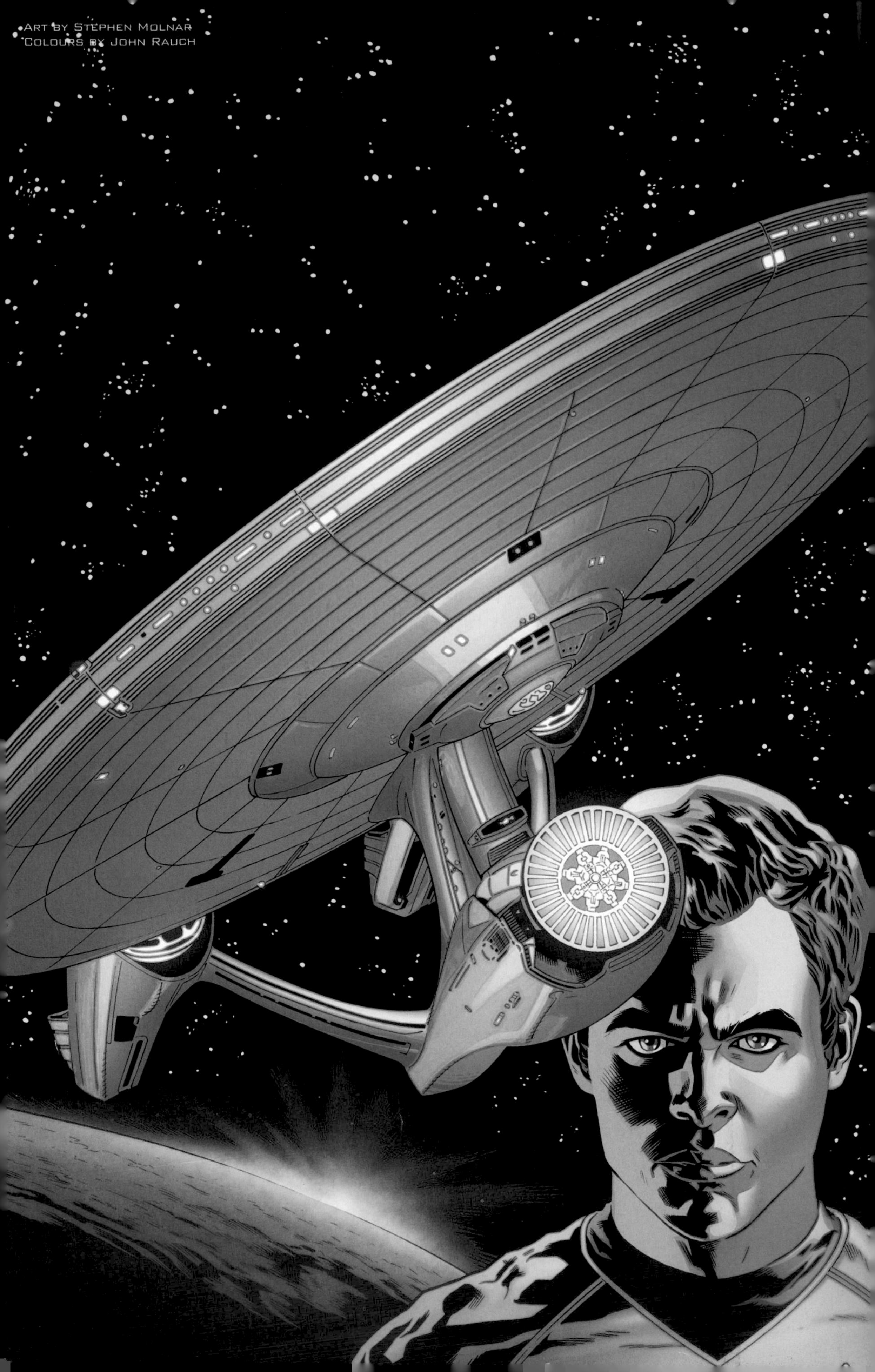

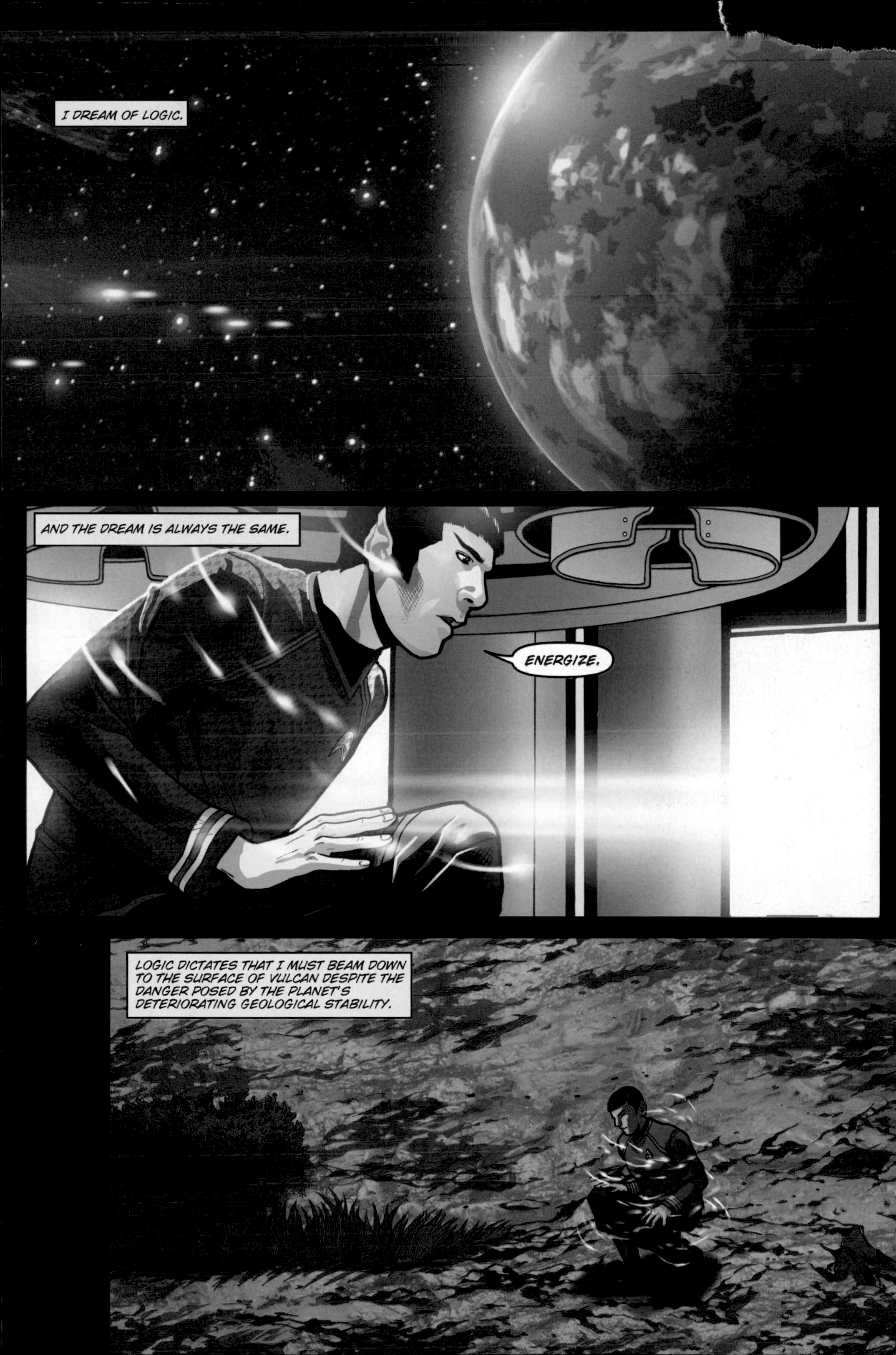
I DREAM OF LOGIC.
AND THE DREAM IS ALWAYS THE SAME.
ENERGIZE.
LOGIC DICTATES THAT I MUST BEAM DOWN TO THE SURFACE OF VULCAN DESPITE THE DANGER POSED BY THE PLANET'S DETERIORATING GEOLOGICAL STABILITY.

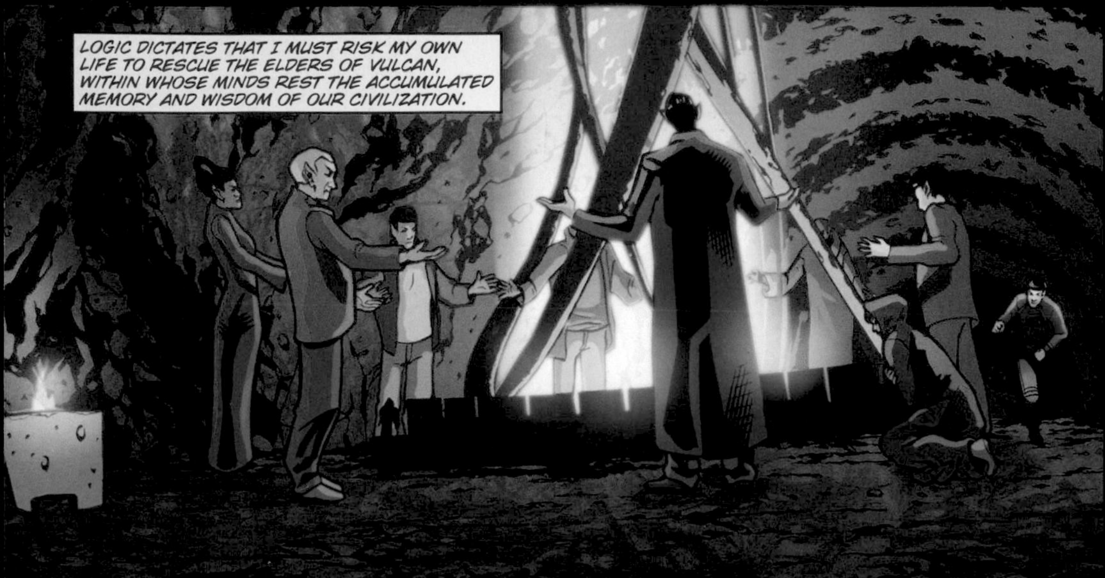
LOGIC DICTATES THAT I MUST RISK MY OWN LIFE TO RESCUE THE ELDERS OF VULCAN, WITHIN WHOSE MINDS REST THE ACCUMULATED MEMORY AND WISDOM OF OUR CIVILIZATION.

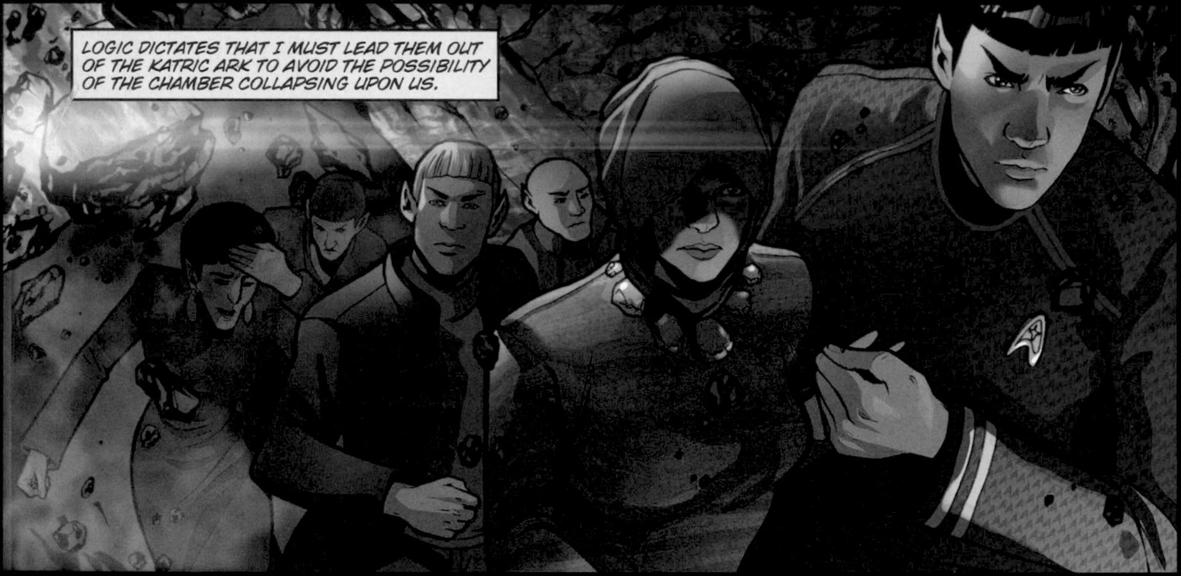
LOGIC DICTATES THAT I MUST LEAD THEM OUT OF THE KATRIC ARK TO AVOID THE POSSIBILITY OF THE CHAMBER COLLAPSING UPON US.

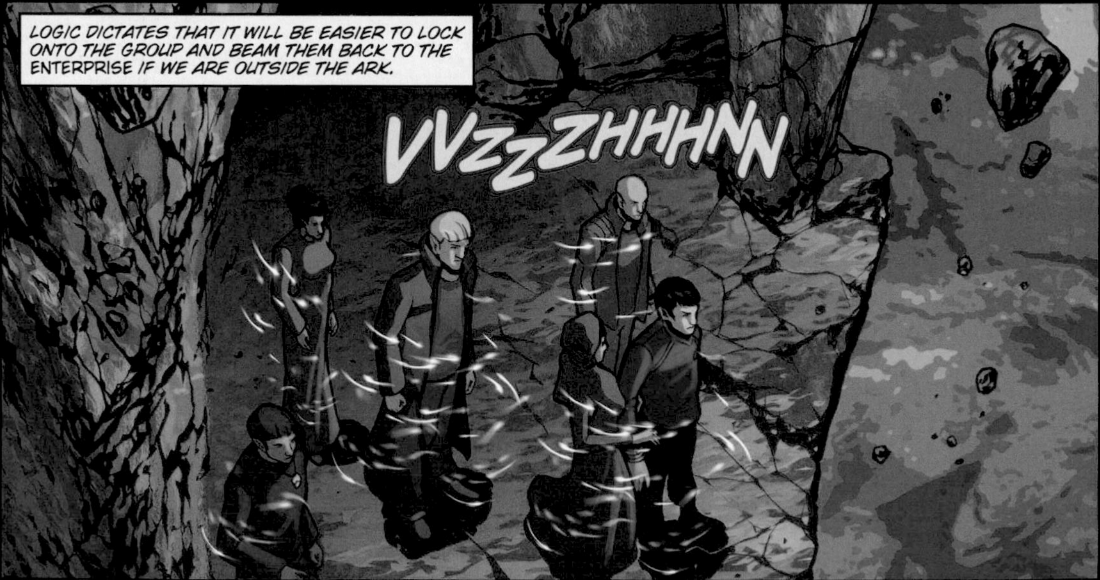
LOGIC DICTATES THAT IT WILL BE EASIER TO LOCK ONTO THE GROUP AND BEAM THEM BACK TO THE ENTERPRISE IF WE ARE OUTSIDE THE ARK.
VVZZZHHHHNN

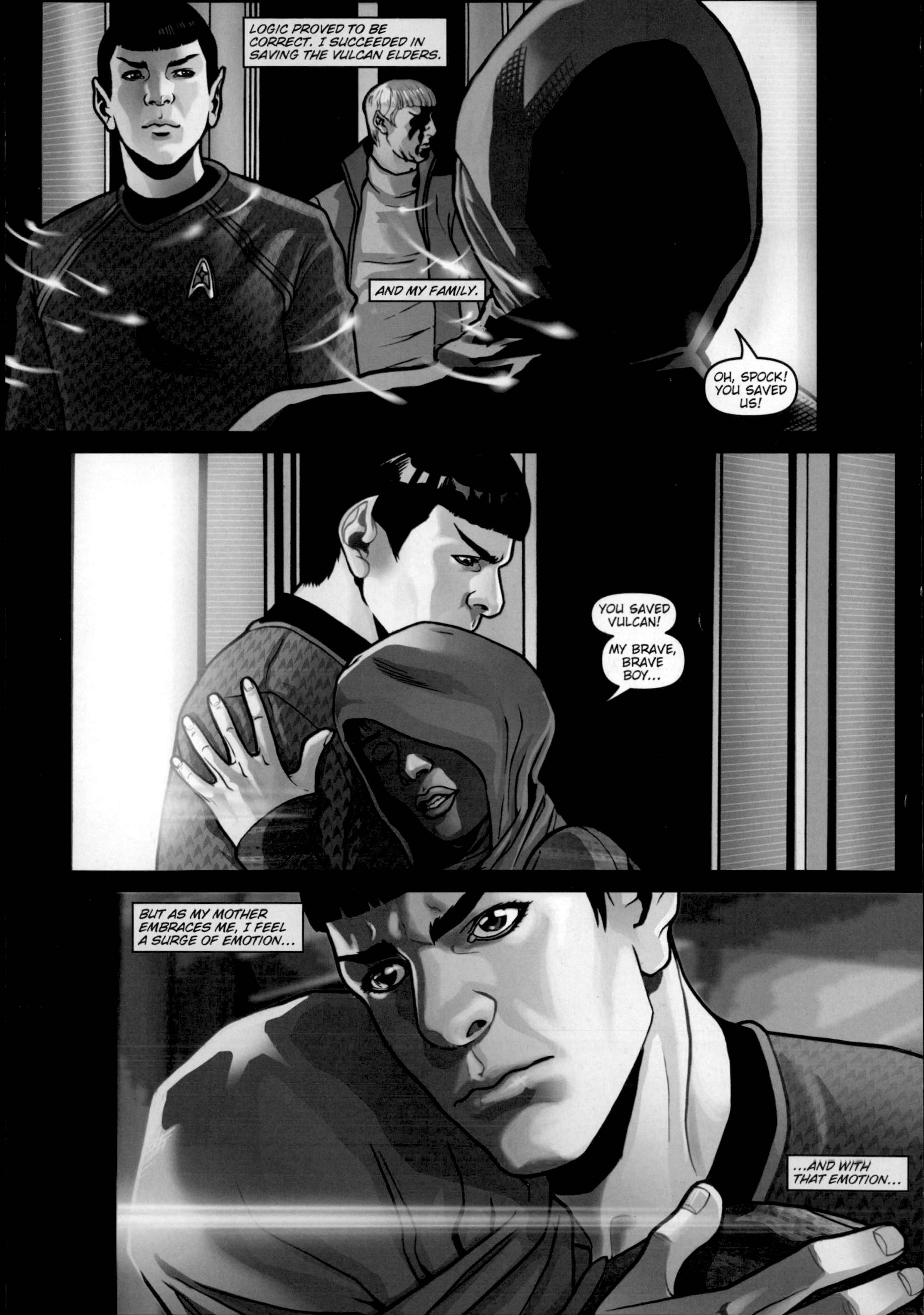
LOGIC PROVED TO BE CORRECT. I SUCCEEDED IN SAVING THE VULCAN ELDERS.
AND MY FAMILY.
OH, SPOCK! YOU SAVED US!
YOU SAVED VULCAN!
MY BRAVE, BRAVE BOY...
BUT AS MY MOTHER EMBRACES ME, I FEEL A SURGE OF EMOTION...
...AND WITH THAT EMOTION...

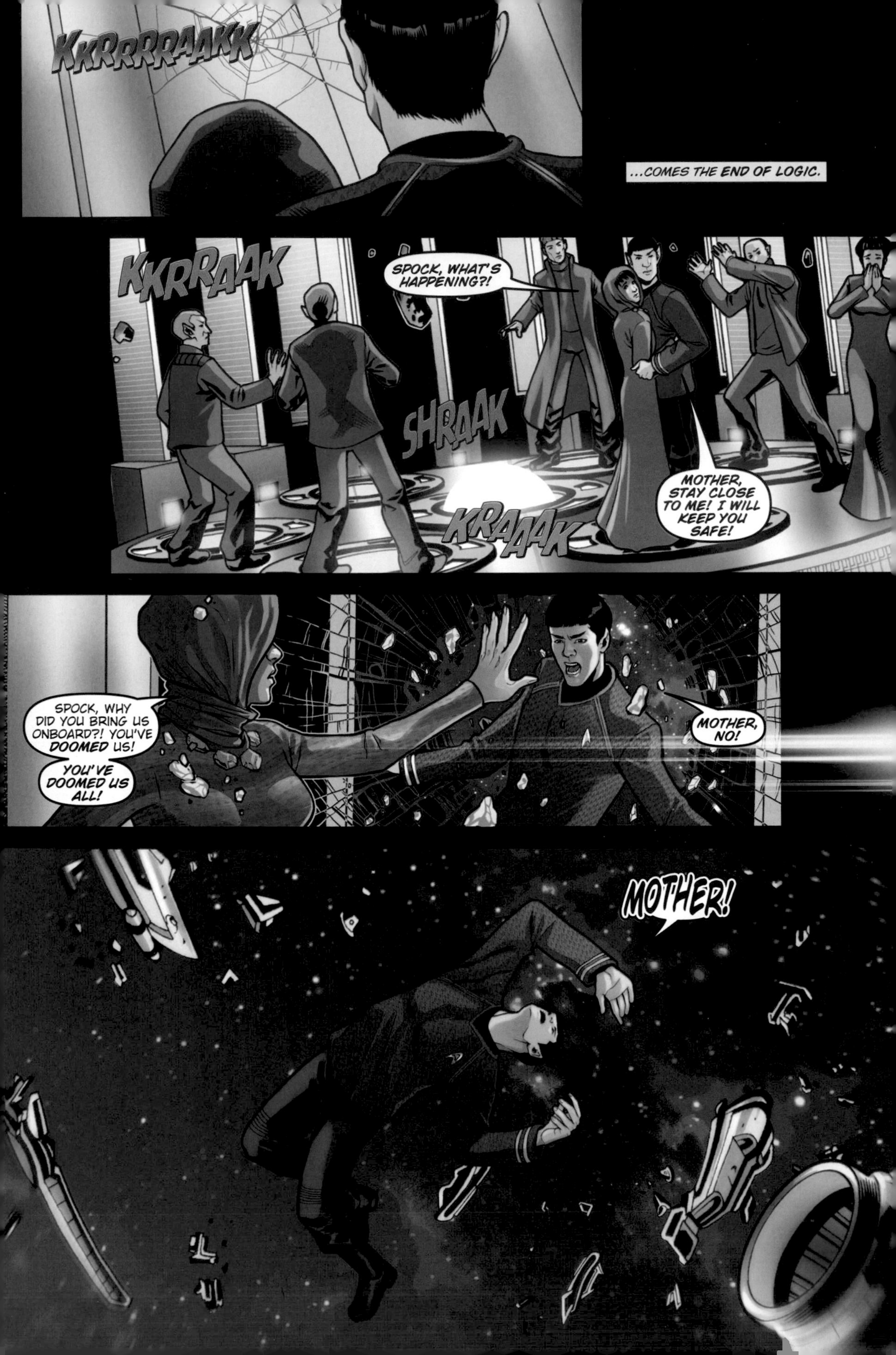
KKRRRRAAKK
...COMES THE END OF LOGIC.
KKRRAAK
SPOCK, WHAT'S HAPPENING?!
SHRAAK
MOTHER, STAY CLOSE TO ME! I WILL KEEP YOU SAFE!
KRAAAK
SPOCK, WHY DID YOU BRING US ONBOARD?! YOU'VE DOOMED US!
YOU'VE DOOMED US ALL!
MOTHER, NO!
MOTHER!

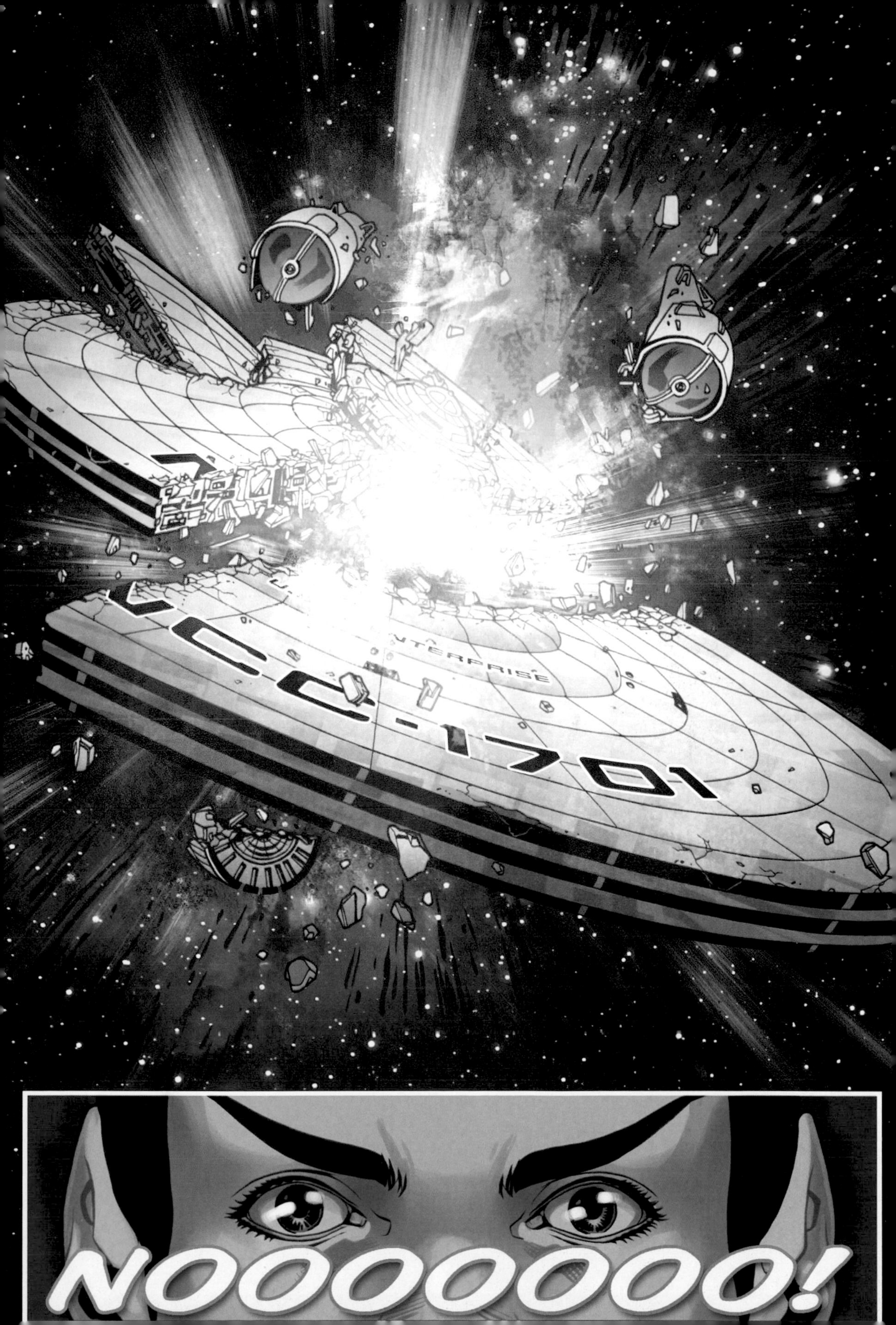
NCC-1701
NTERPRISE
NOOOOOOO!

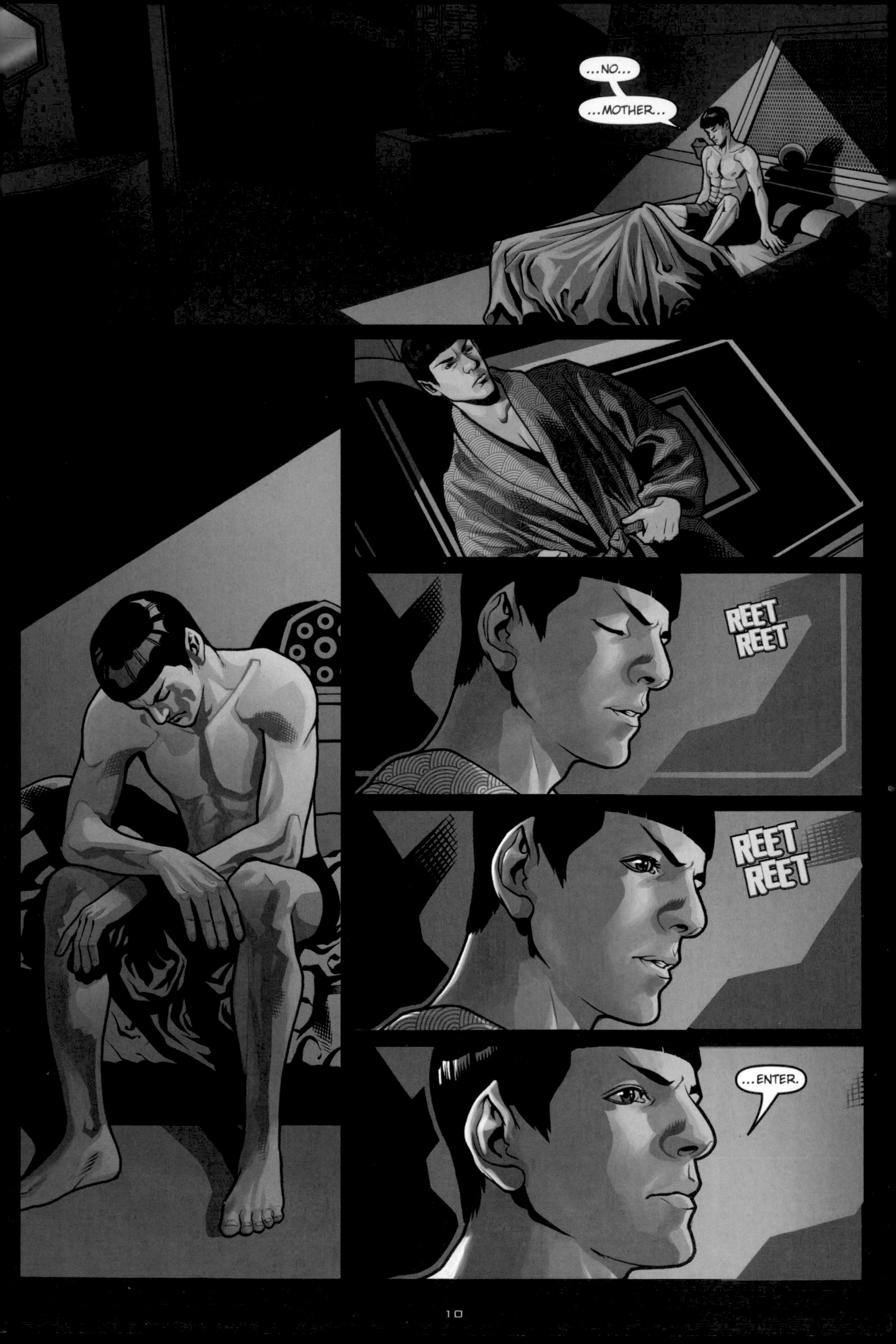
...NO...
...MOTHER...
REET REET
REET REET
...ENTER.

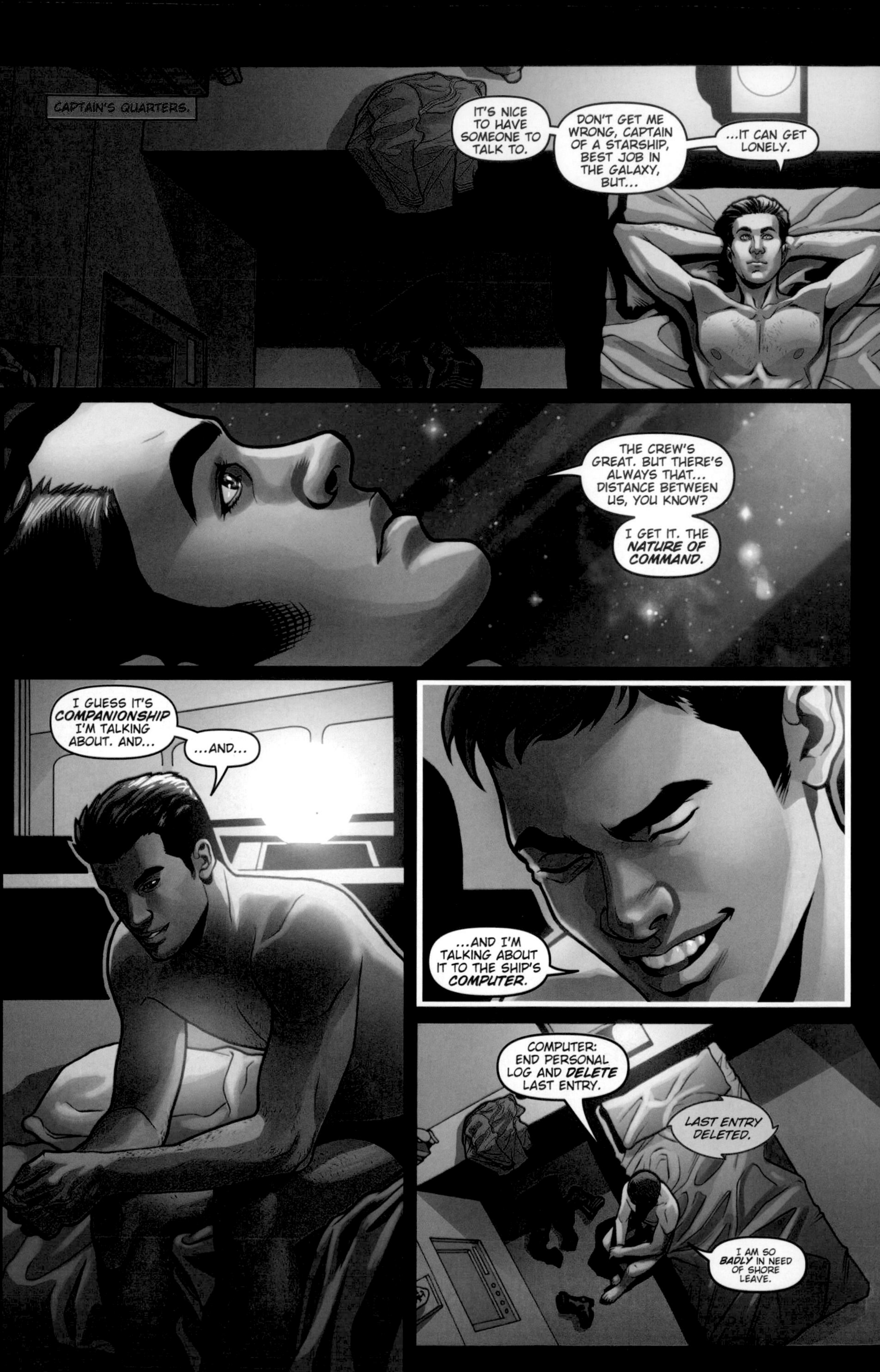
CAPTAIN'S QUARTERS.
IT'S NICE TO HAVE SOMEONE TO TALK TO.
DON'T GET ME WRONG, CAPTAIN OF A STARSHIP, BEST JOB IN THE GALAXY, BUT...
...IT CAN GET LONELY.
THE CREW'S GREAT. BUT THERE'S ALWAYS THAT... DISTANCE BETWEEN US, YOU KNOW?
I GET IT. THE NATURE OF COMMAND.
I GUESS IT'S COMPANIONSHIP I'M TALKING ABOUT. AND...
...AND...
...AND I'M TALKING ABOUT IT TO THE SHIP'S COMPUTER.
COMPUTER: END PERSONAL LOG AND DELETE LAST ENTRY.
LAST ENTRY DELETED.
I AM SO BADLY IN NEED OF SHORE LEAVE.

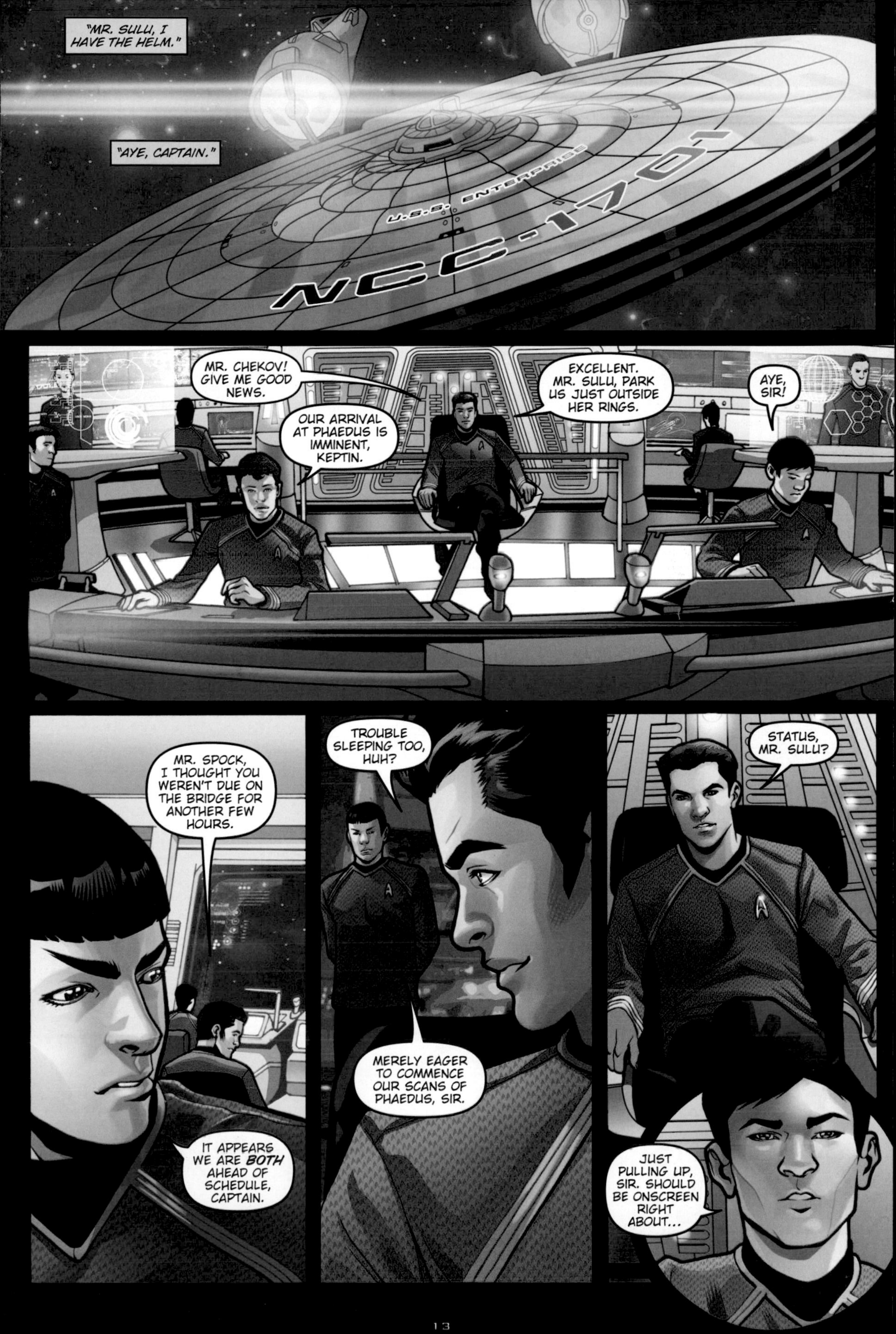
"MR. SULU, I HAVE THE HELM."
"AYE, CAPTAIN."
U.S.S. ENTERPRISE
NCC-1701
MR. CHEKOV! GIVE ME GOOD NEWS.
OUR ARRIVAL AT PHAEDUS IS IMMINENT, KEPTIN.
EXCELLENT. MR. SULU, PARK US JUST OUTSIDE HER RINGS.
AYE, SIR!
MR. SPOCK, I THOUGHT YOU WEREN'T DUE ON THE BRIDGE FOR ANOTHER FEW HOURS.
IT APPEARS WE ARE *BOTH* AHEAD OF SCHEDULE, CAPTAIN.
TROUBLE SLEEPING TOO, HUH?
MERELY EAGER TO COMMENCE OUR SCANS OF PHAEDUS, SIR.
STATUS, MR. SULU?
JUST PULLING UP, SIR. SHOULD BE ONSCREEN RIGHT ABOUT...

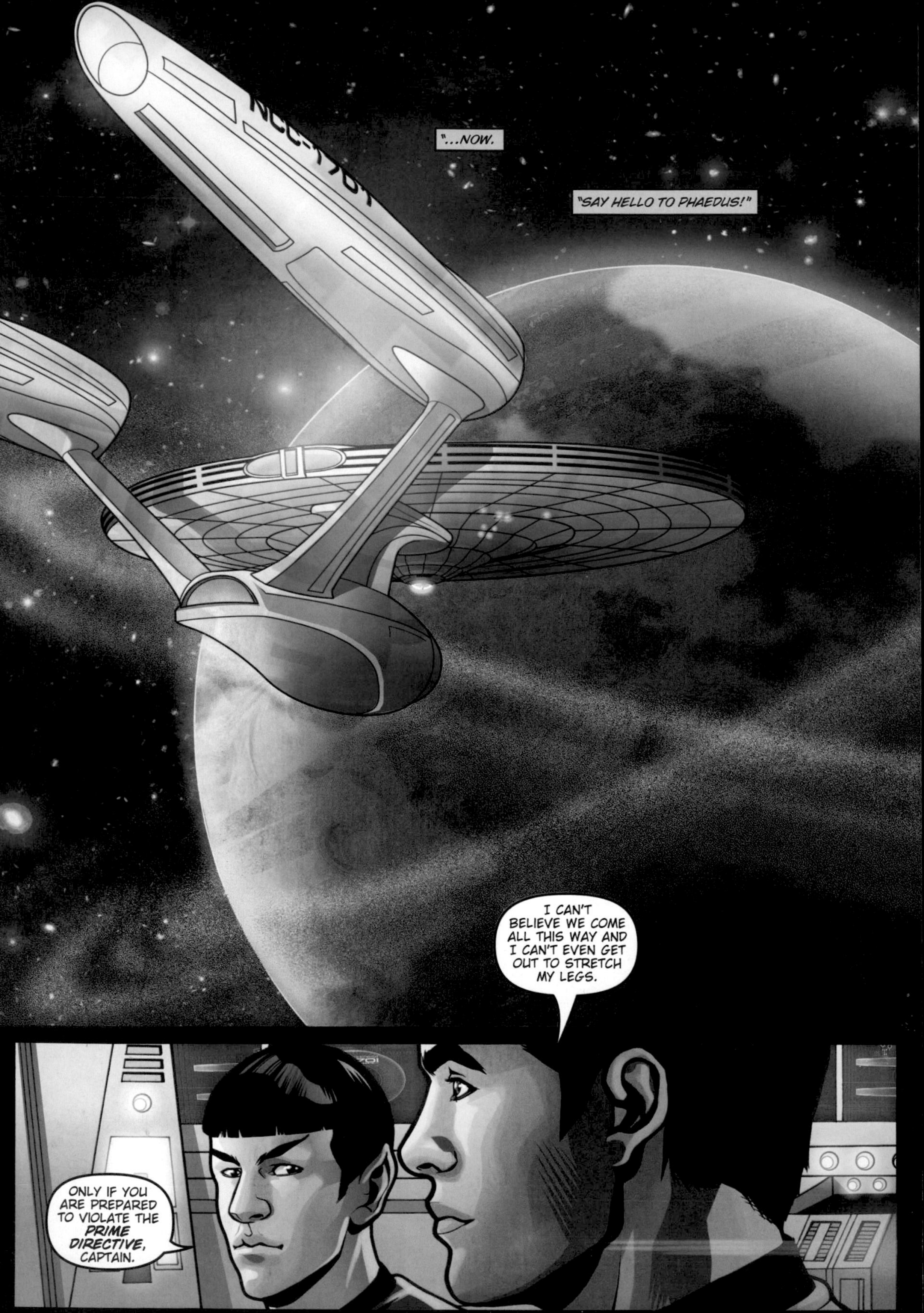
"...NOW.
"SAY HELLO TO PHAEDUS!"
I CAN'T BELIEVE WE COME ALL THIS WAY AND I CAN'T EVEN GET OUT TO STRETCH MY LEGS.
ONLY IF YOU ARE PREPARED TO VIOLATE THE PRIME DIRECTIVE, CAPTAIN.

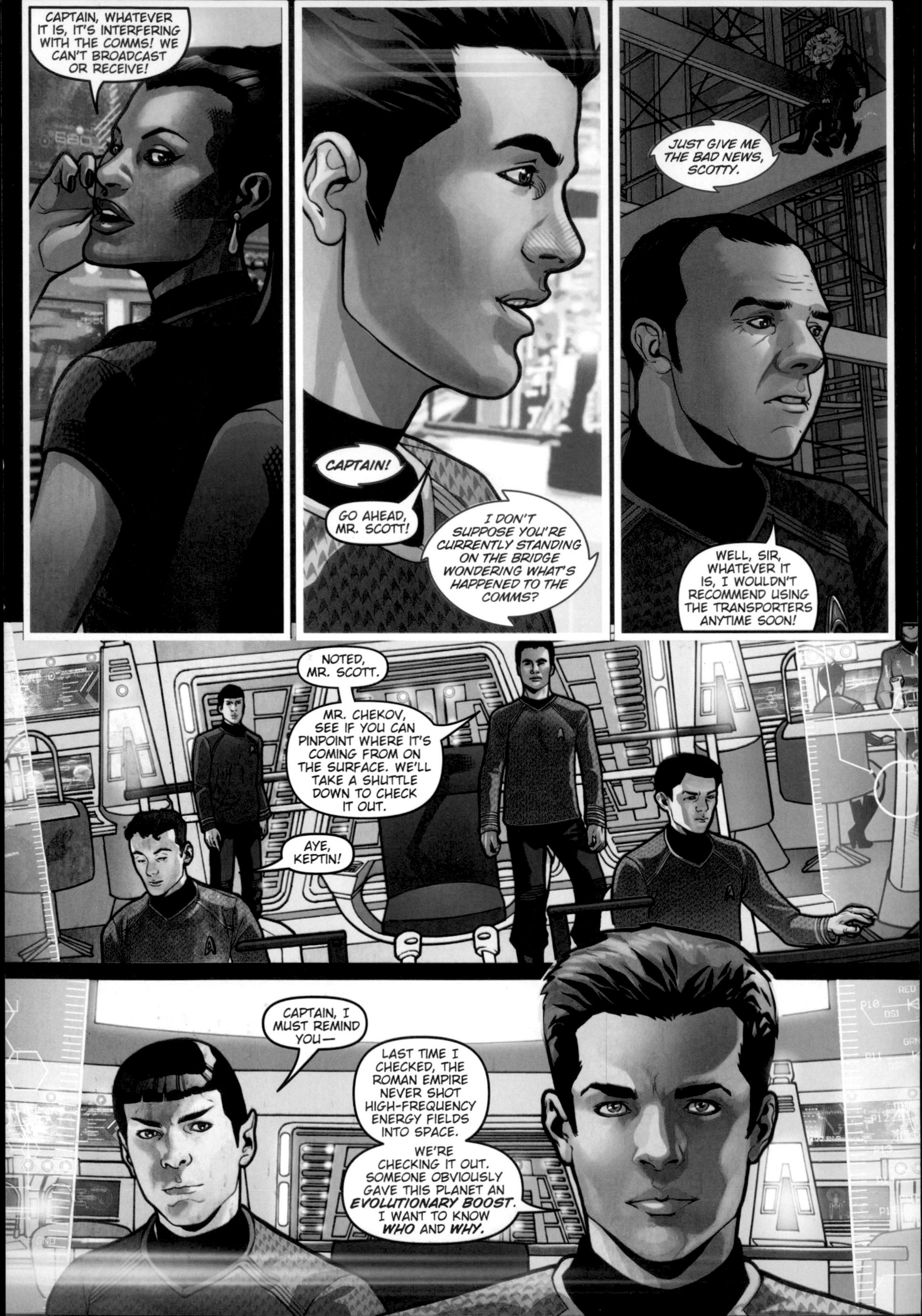
CAPTAIN, WHATEVER IT IS, IT'S INTERFERING WITH THE COMMS! WE CAN'T BROADCAST OR RECEIVE!
CAPTAIN!
GO AHEAD, MR. SCOTT!
I DON'T SUPPOSE YOU'RE CURRENTLY STANDING ON THE BRIDGE WONDERING WHAT'S HAPPENED TO THE COMMS?
JUST GIVE ME THE BAD NEWS, SCOTTY.
WELL, SIR, WHATEVER IT IS, I WOULDN'T RECOMMEND USING THE TRANSPORTERS ANYTIME SOON!
NOTED, MR. SCOTT.
MR. CHEKOV, SEE IF YOU CAN PINPOINT WHERE IT'S COMING FROM ON THE SURFACE. WE'LL TAKE A SHUTTLE DOWN TO CHECK IT OUT.
AYE, KEPTIN!
CAPTAIN, I MUST REMIND YOU—
LAST TIME I CHECKED, THE ROMAN EMPIRE NEVER SHOT HIGH-FREQUENCY ENERGY FIELDS INTO SPACE.
WE'RE CHECKING IT OUT. SOMEONE OBVIOUSLY GAVE THIS PLANET AN EVOLUTIONARY BOOST. I WANT TO KNOW WHO AND WHY.

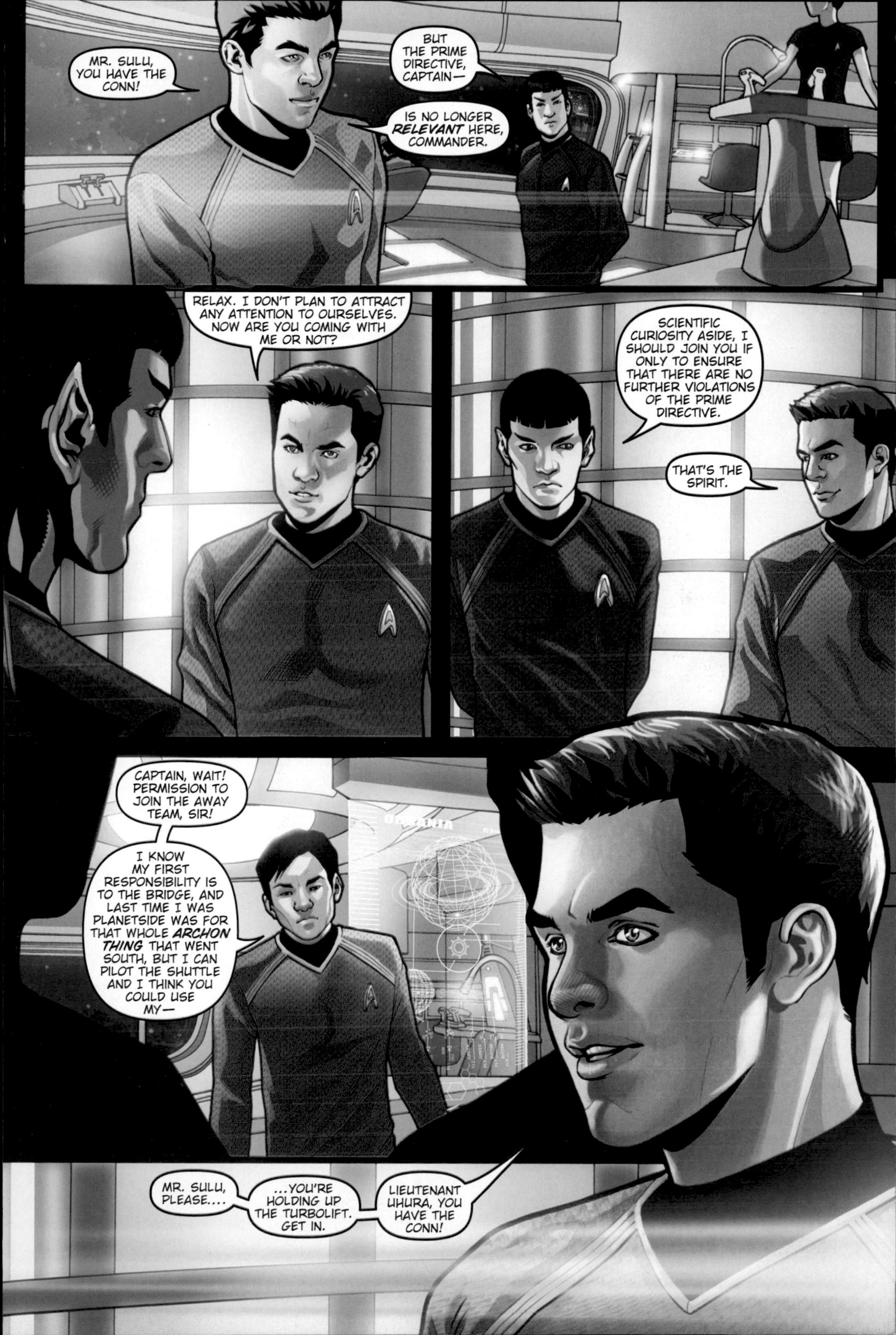
MR. SULU, YOU HAVE THE CONN!
BUT THE PRIME DIRECTIVE, CAPTAIN—
IS NO LONGER RELEVANT HERE, COMMANDER.
RELAX. I DON'T PLAN TO ATTRACT ANY ATTENTION TO OURSELVES. NOW ARE YOU COMING WITH ME OR NOT?
SCIENTIFIC CURIOSITY ASIDE, I SHOULD JOIN YOU IF ONLY TO ENSURE THAT THERE ARE NO FURTHER VIOLATIONS OF THE PRIME DIRECTIVE.
THAT'S THE SPIRIT.
CAPTAIN, WAIT! PERMISSION TO JOIN THE AWAY TEAM, SIR!
I KNOW MY FIRST RESPONSIBILITY IS TO THE BRIDGE, AND LAST TIME I WAS PLANETSIDE WAS FOR THAT WHOLE ARCHON THING THAT WENT SOUTH, BUT I CAN PILOT THE SHUTTLE AND I THINK YOU COULD USE MY—
MR. SULU, PLEASE....
...YOU'RE HOLDING UP THE TURBOLIFT. GET IN.
LIEUTENANT UHURA, YOU HAVE THE CONN!

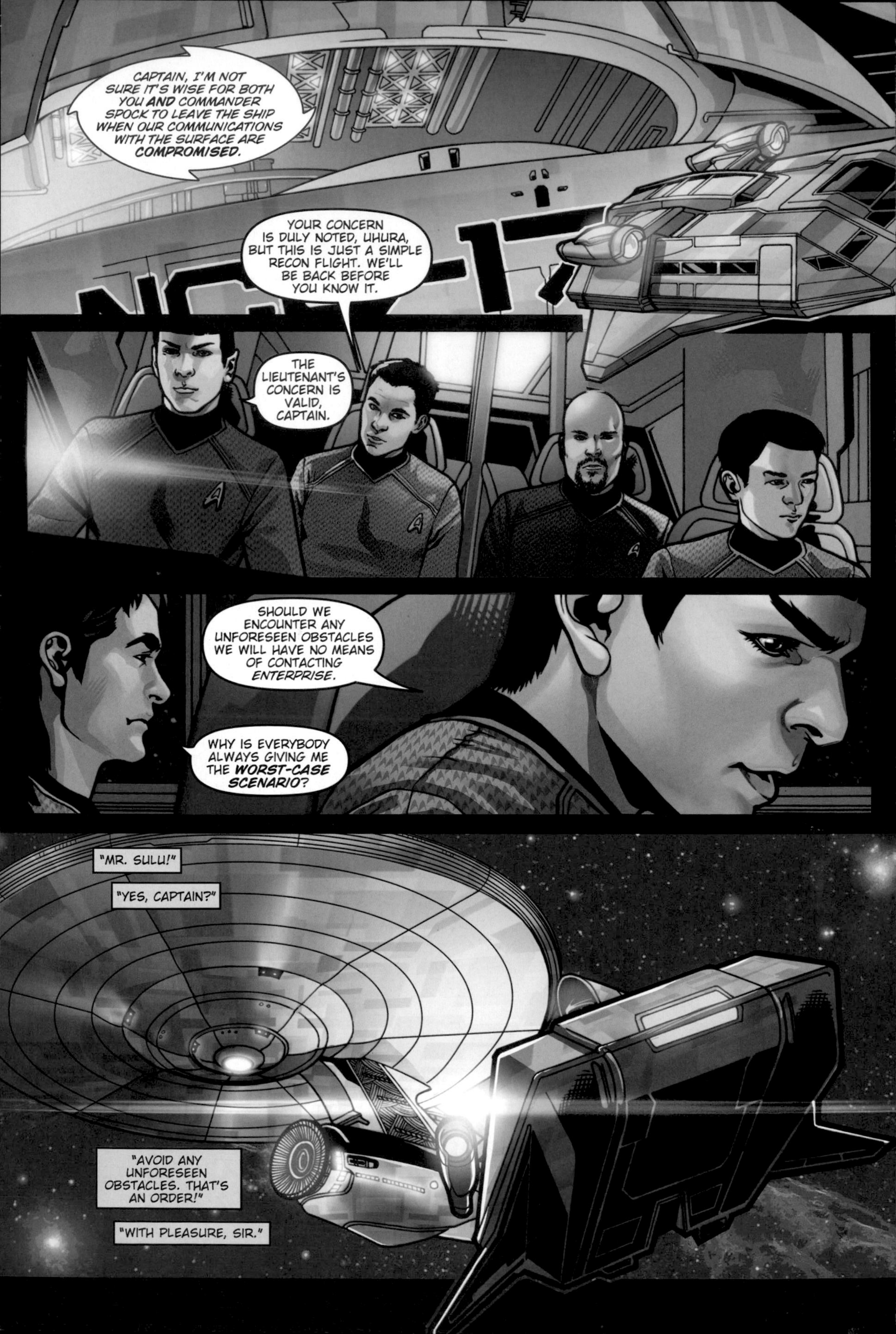
CAPTAIN, I'M NOT SURE IT'S WISE FOR BOTH YOU **AND** COMMANDER SPOCK TO LEAVE THE SHIP WHEN OUR COMMUNICATIONS WITH THE SURFACE ARE **COMPROMISED**.
YOUR CONCERN IS DULY NOTED, UHURA, BUT THIS IS JUST A SIMPLE RECON FLIGHT. WE'LL BE BACK BEFORE YOU KNOW IT.
NCC-17
THE LIEUTENANT'S CONCERN IS VALID, CAPTAIN.
SHOULD WE ENCOUNTER ANY UNFORESEEN OBSTACLES WE WILL HAVE NO MEANS OF CONTACTING *ENTERPRISE*.
WHY IS EVERYBODY ALWAYS GIVING ME THE ***WORST-CASE SCENARIO***?
"MR. SULU!"
"YES, CAPTAIN?"
"AVOID ANY UNFORESEEN OBSTACLES. THAT'S AN ORDER!"
"WITH PLEASURE, SIR."

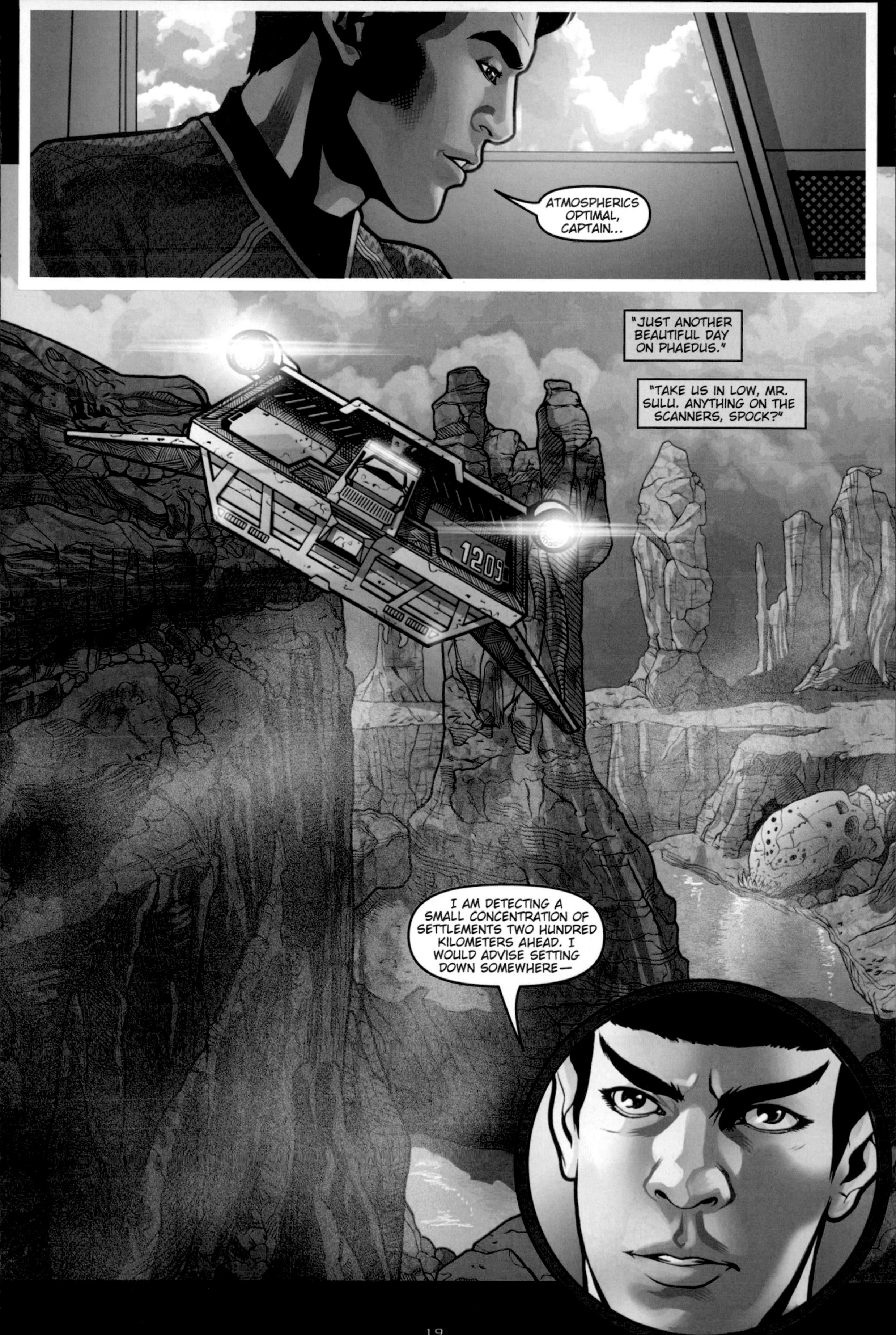
ATMOSPHERICS OPTIMAL, CAPTAIN...
"JUST ANOTHER BEAUTIFUL DAY ON PHAEDUS."
"TAKE US IN LOW, MR. SULU. ANYTHING ON THE SCANNERS, SPOCK?"
I AM DETECTING A SMALL CONCENTRATION OF SETTLEMENTS TWO HUNDRED KILOMETERS AHEAD. I WOULD ADVISE SETTING DOWN SOMEWHERE—

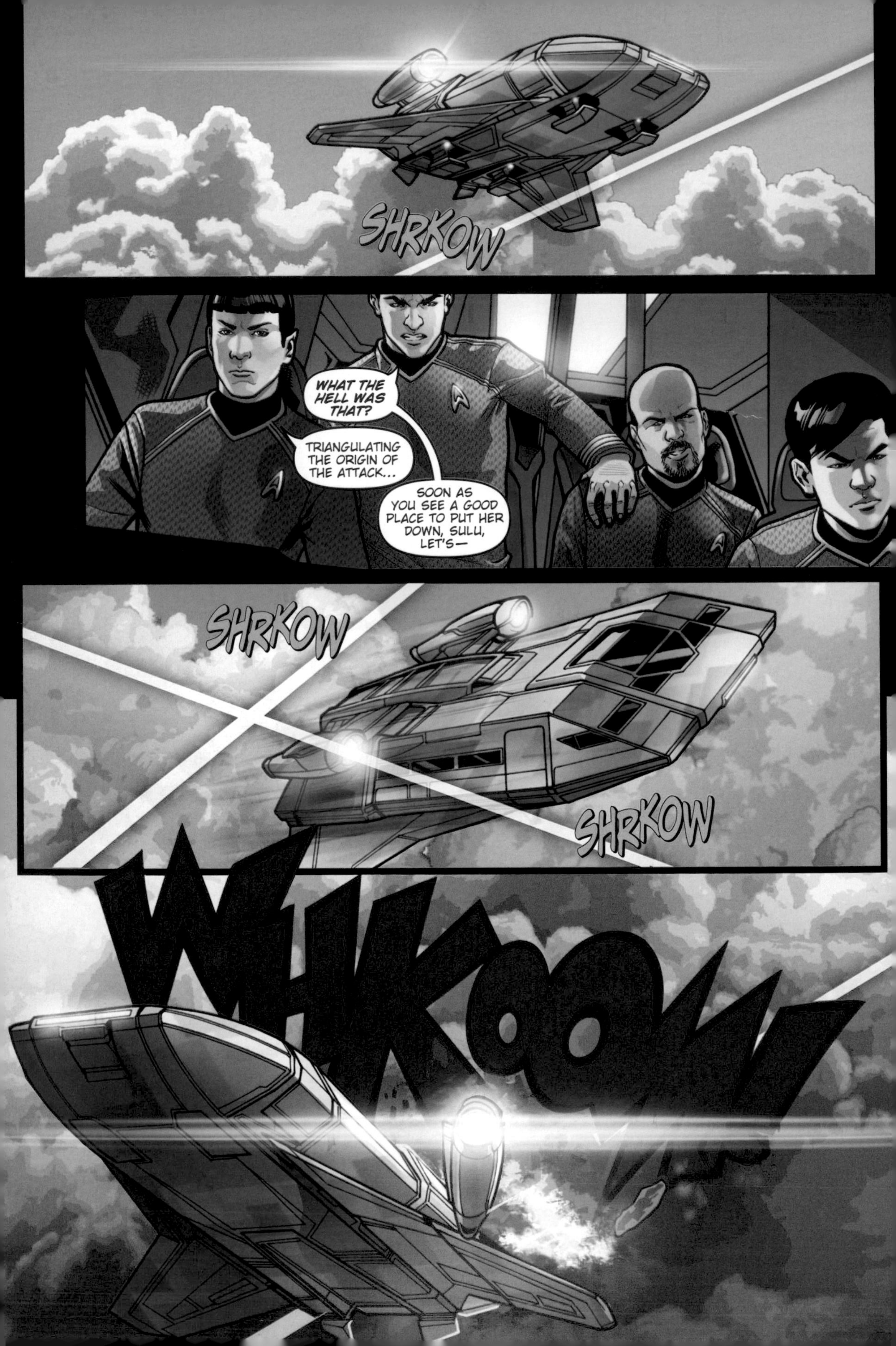
SHRKOW
WHAT THE HELL WAS THAT?
TRIANGULATING THE ORIGIN OF THE ATTACK...
SOON AS YOU SEE A GOOD PLACE TO PUT HER DOWN, SULU, LET'S—
SHRKOW
SHRKOW
WHKOOM

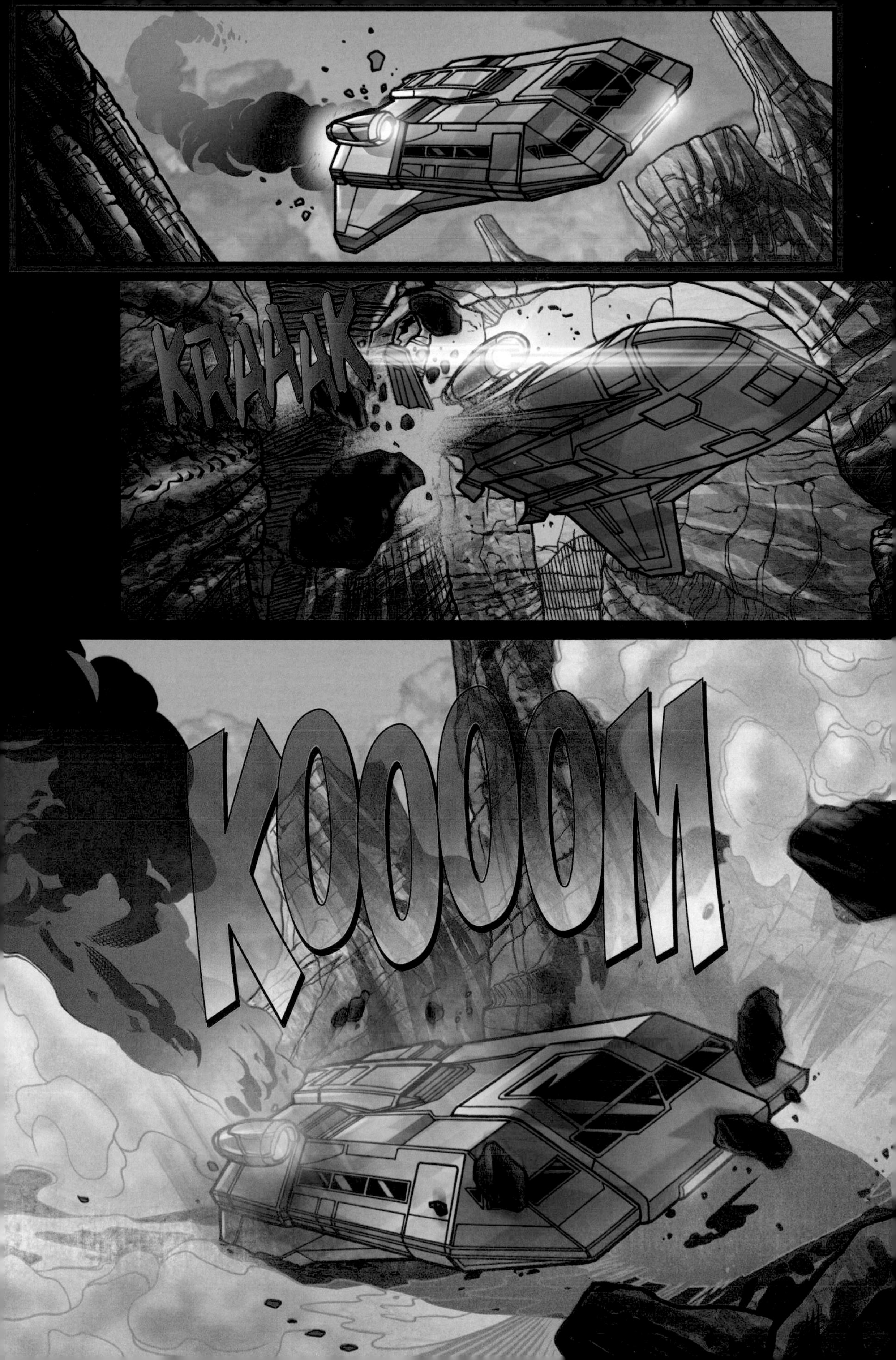
KRAAAK
KOOOOM

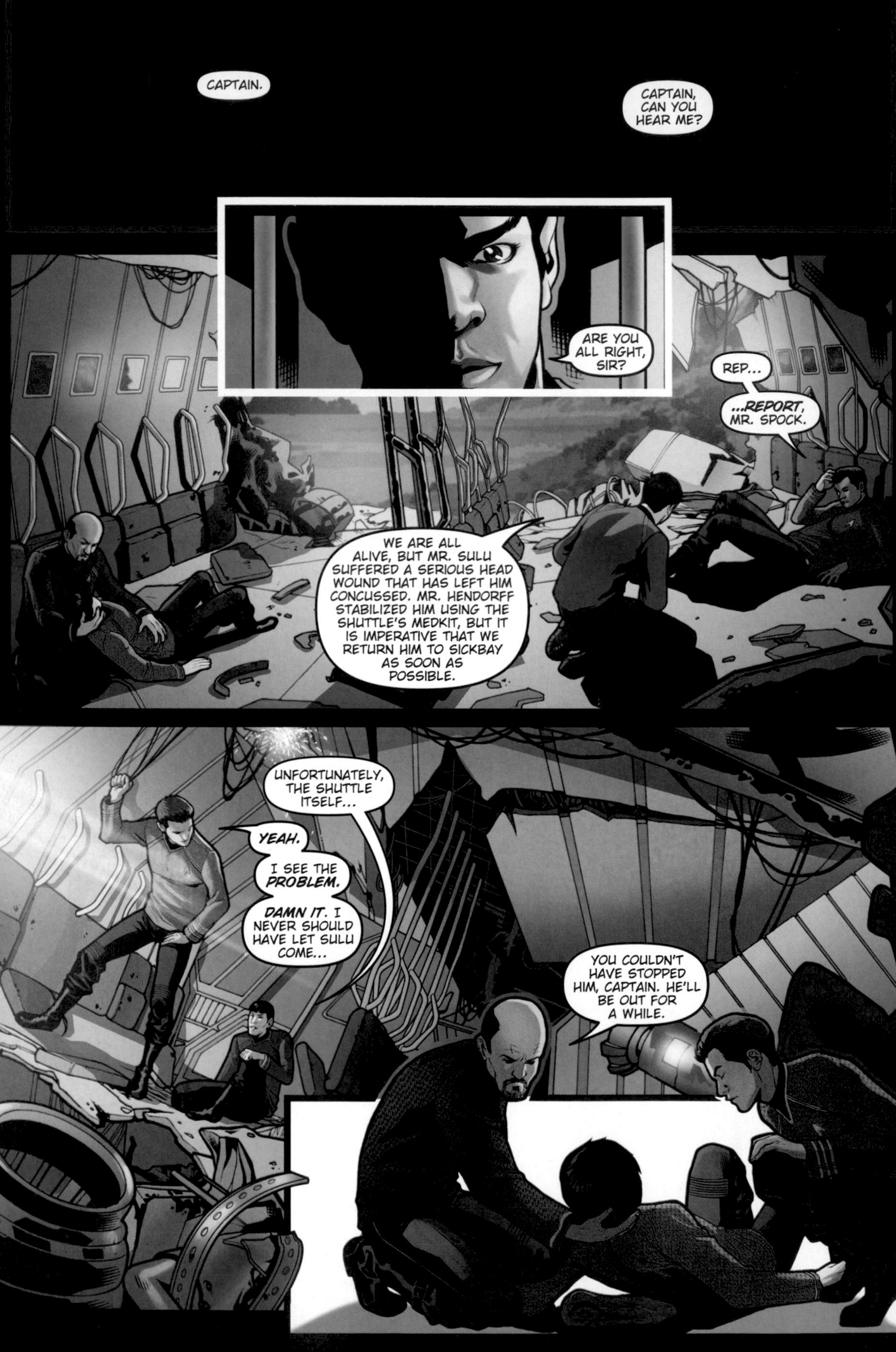
CAPTAIN.
CAPTAIN, CAN YOU HEAR ME?
ARE YOU ALL RIGHT, SIR?
REP...
...REPORT, MR. SPOCK.
WE ARE ALL ALIVE, BUT MR. SULU SUFFERED A SERIOUS HEAD WOUND THAT HAS LEFT HIM CONCUSSED. MR. HENDORFF STABILIZED HIM USING THE SHUTTLE'S MEDKIT, BUT IT IS IMPERATIVE THAT WE RETURN HIM TO SICKBAY AS SOON AS POSSIBLE.
UNFORTUNATELY, THE SHUTTLE ITSELF...
YEAH.
I SEE THE PROBLEM.
DAMN IT. I NEVER SHOULD HAVE LET SULU COME...
YOU COULDN'T HAVE STOPPED HIM, CAPTAIN. HE'LL BE OUT FOR A WHILE.

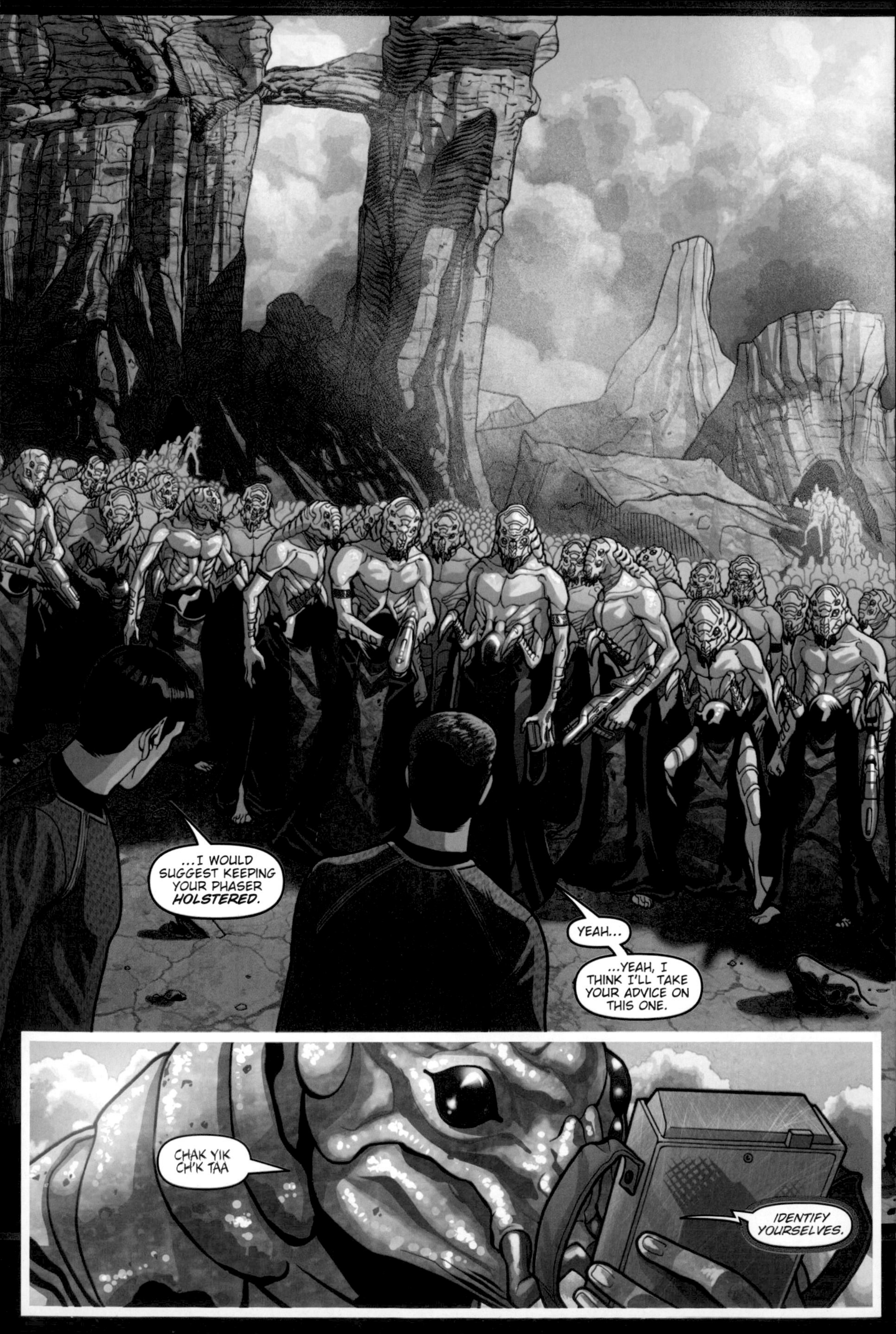
...I WOULD SUGGEST KEEPING YOUR PHASER *HOLSTERED*.
YEAH...
...YEAH, I THINK I'LL TAKE YOUR ADVICE ON THIS ONE.
CHAK YIK CH'K TAA
IDENTIFY YOURSELVES.

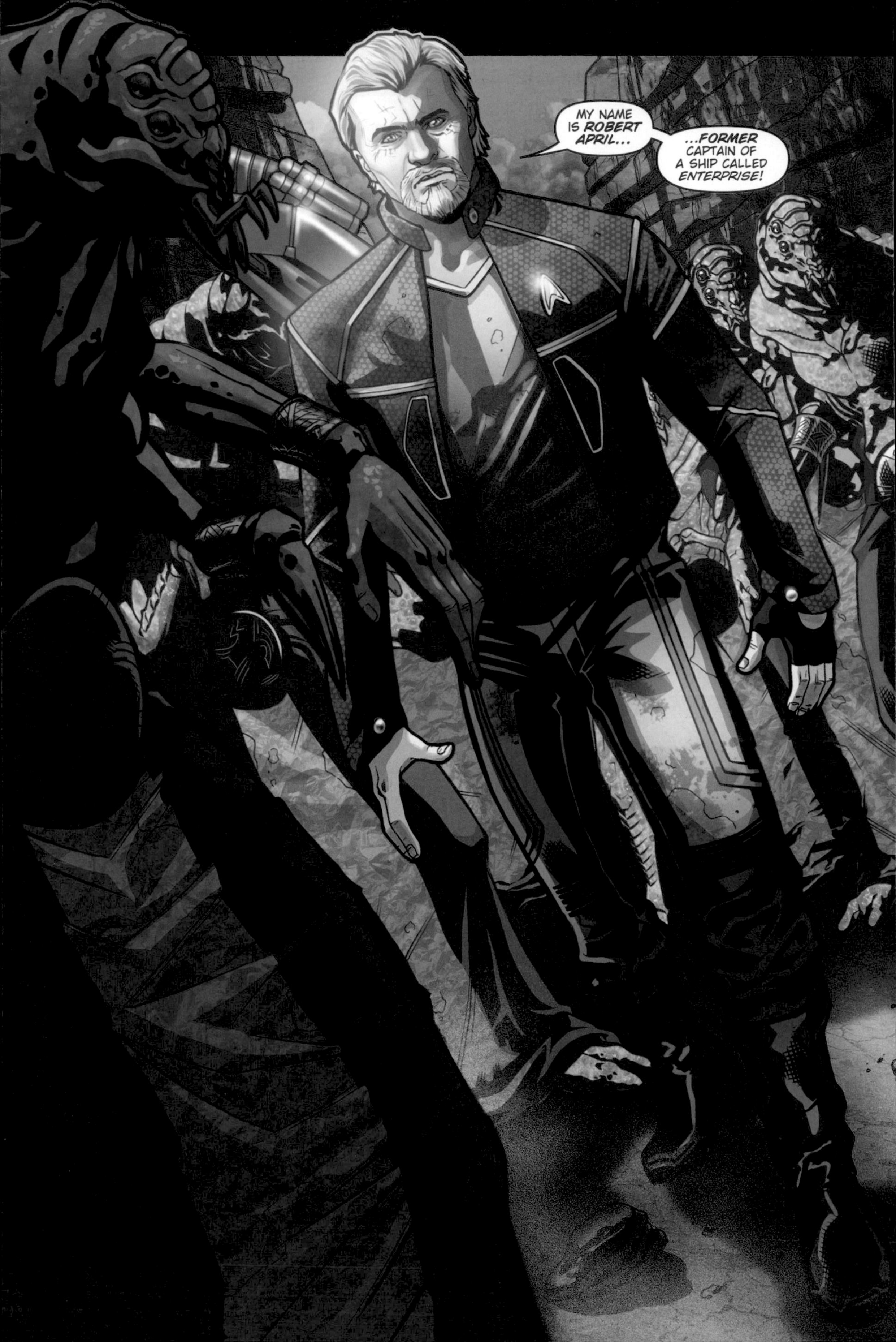
MY NAME IS ROBERT APRIL...
...FORMER CAPTAIN OF A SHIP CALLED ENTERPRISE!

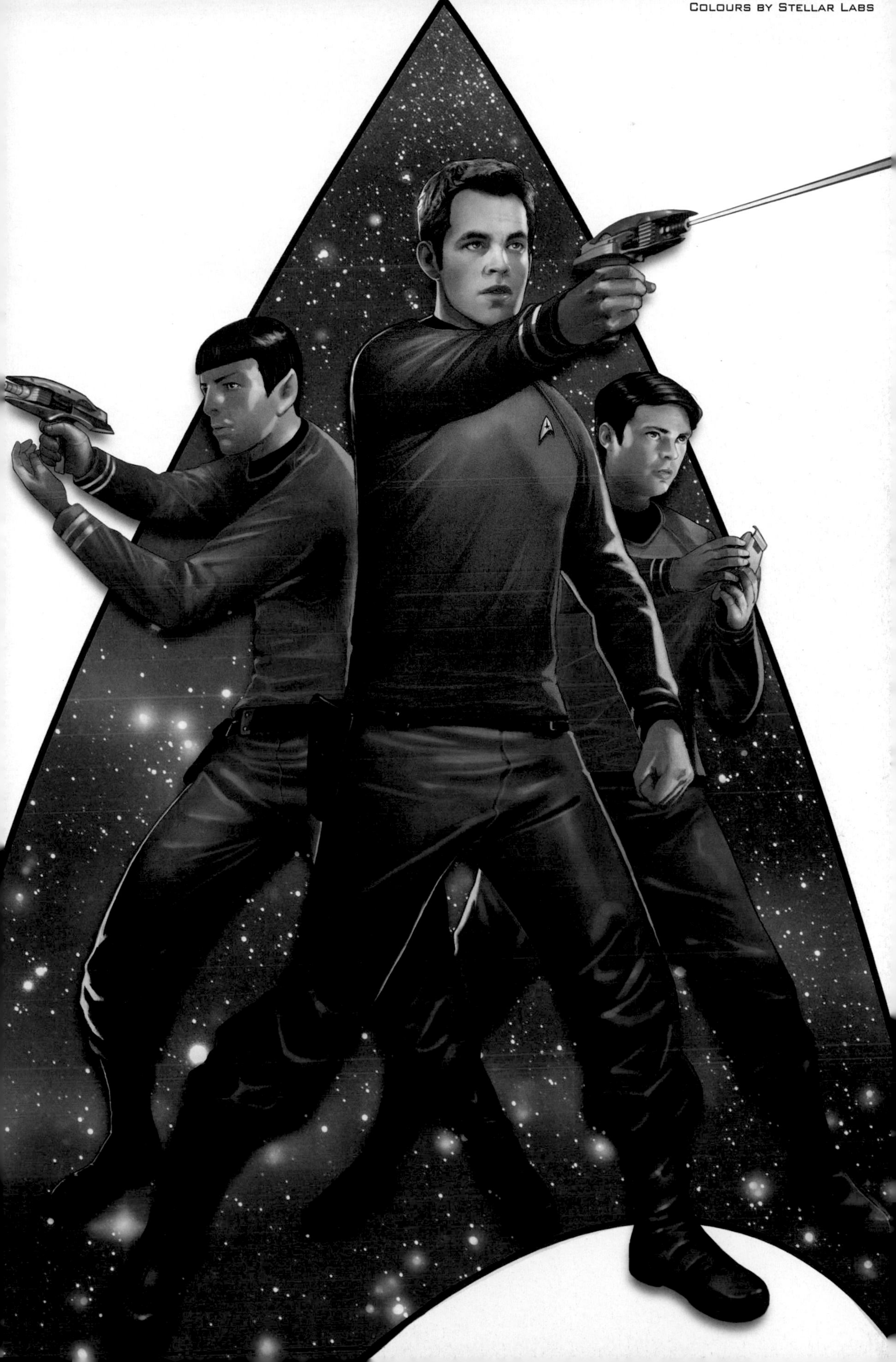

Art by Erfan Fajar
Colours by Stellar Labs

Art by David Messina
Colours by Claudia Scarletgothica

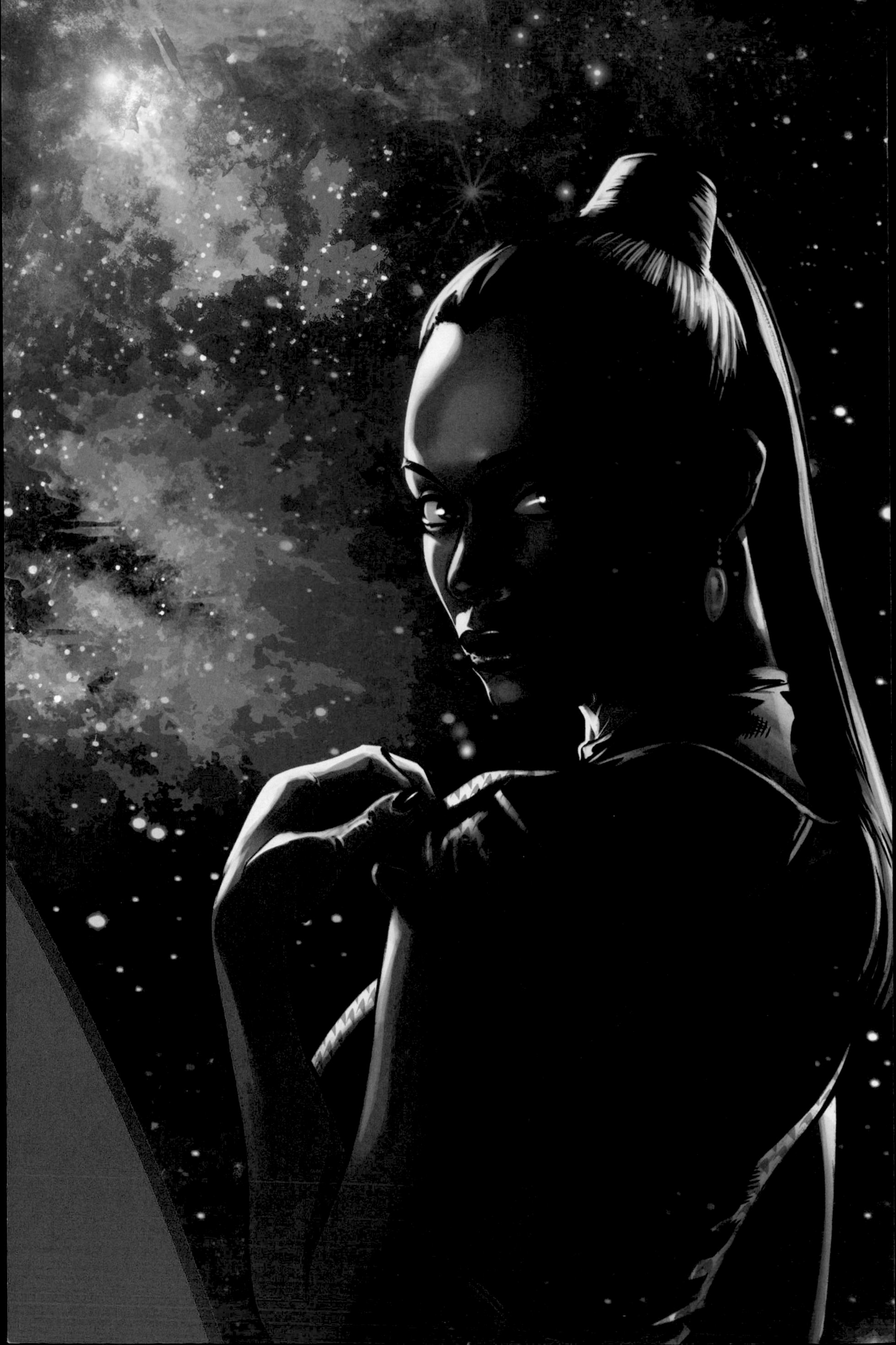

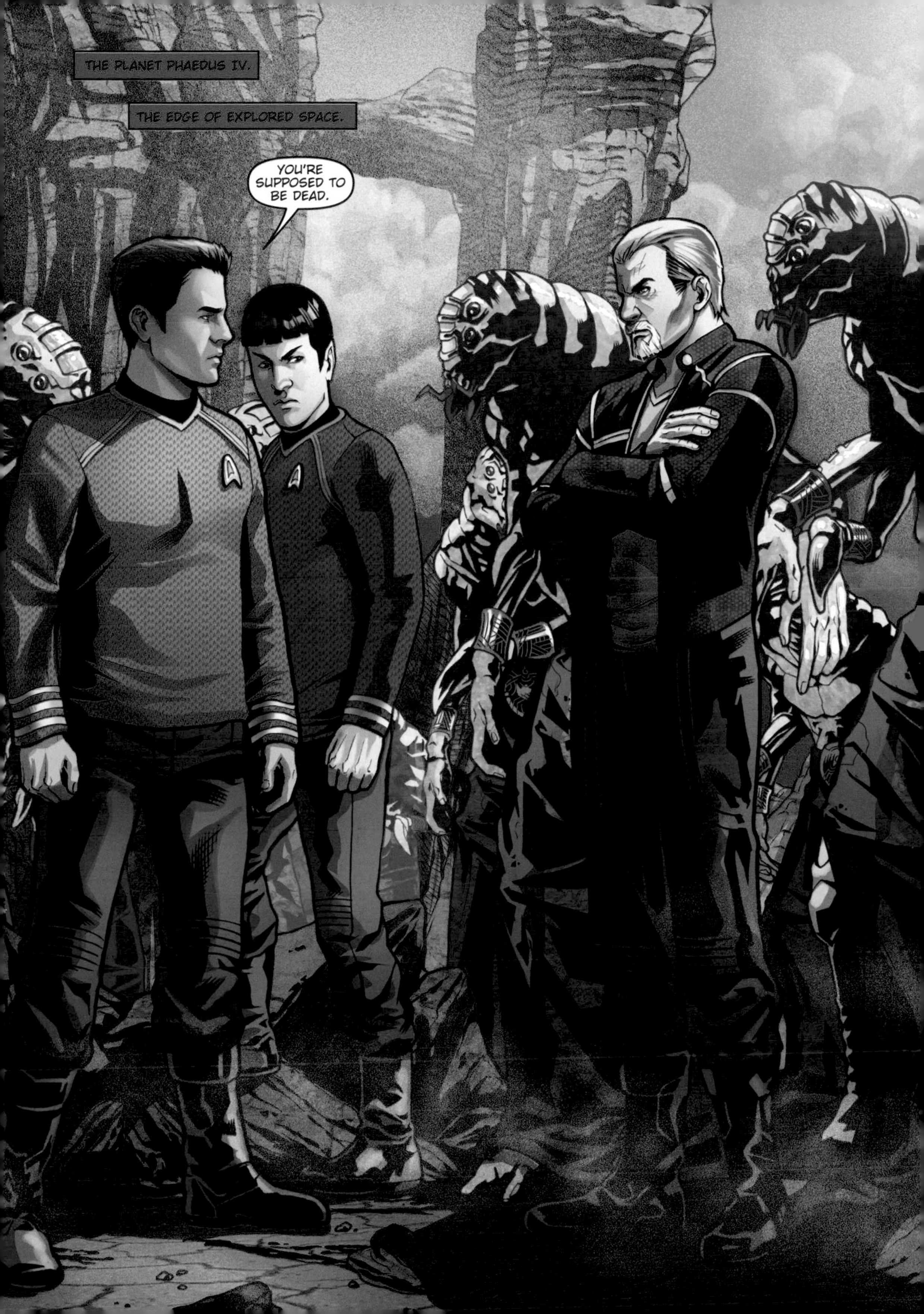
THE PLANET PHAEDUS IV.
THE EDGE OF EXPLORED SPACE.
YOU'RE SUPPOSED TO BE DEAD.

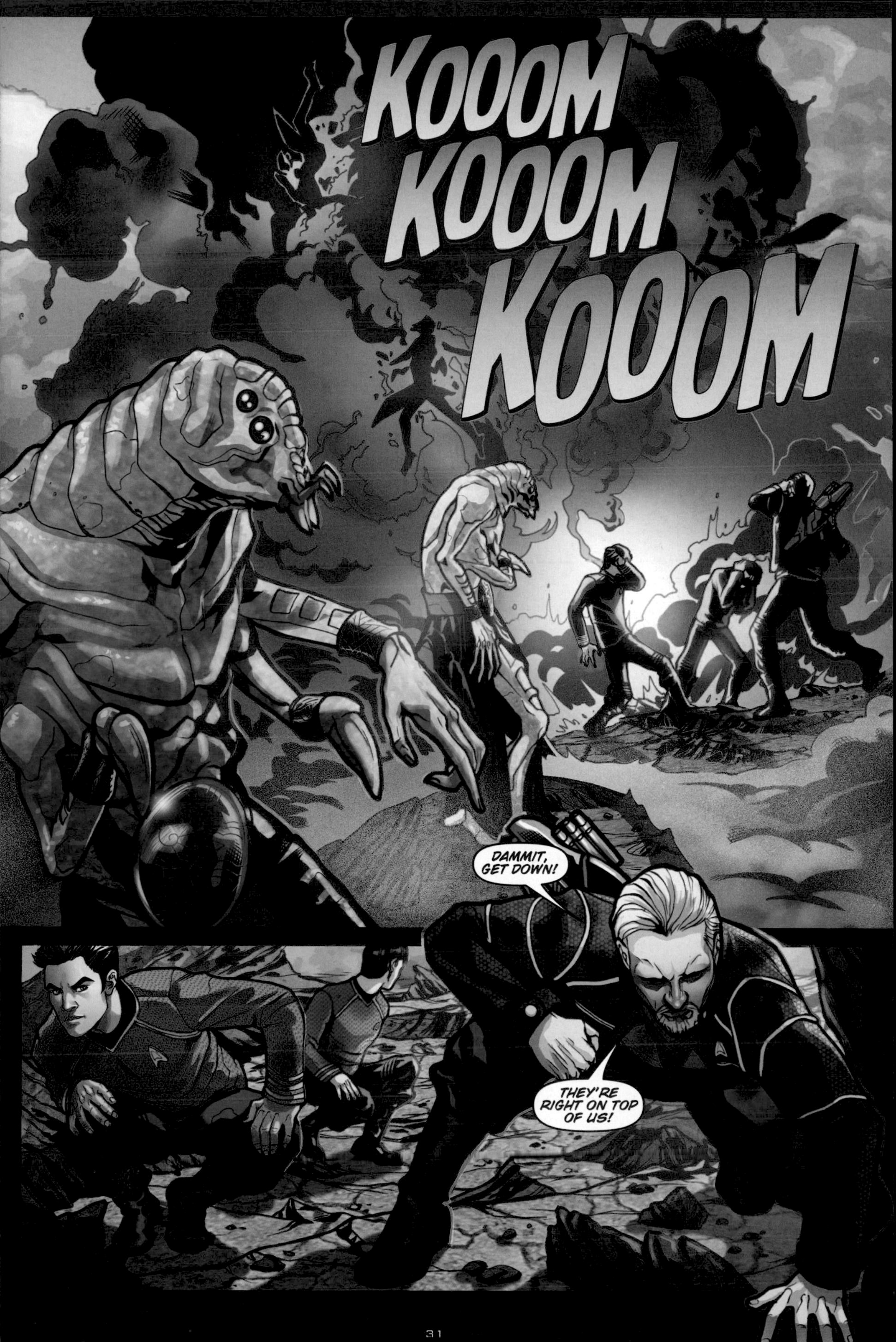
KOOOM
KOOOM
KOOOM
DAMMIT, GET DOWN!
THEY'RE RIGHT ON TOP OF US!

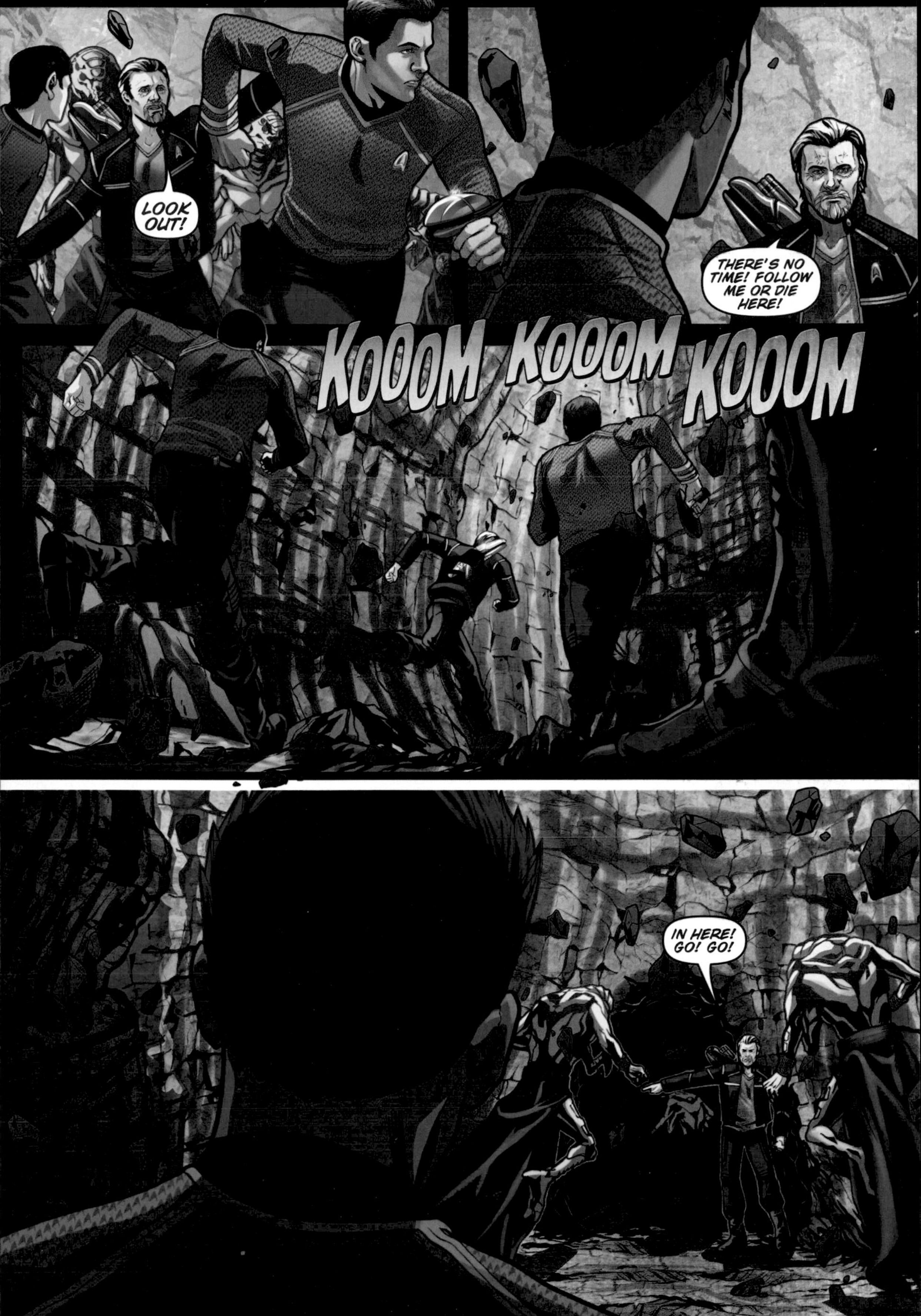
LOOK OUT!
THERE'S NO TIME! FOLLOW ME OR DIE HERE!
KOOOM KOOOM KOOOM
IN HERE! GO! GO!

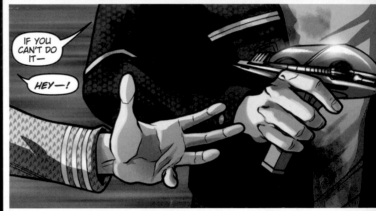

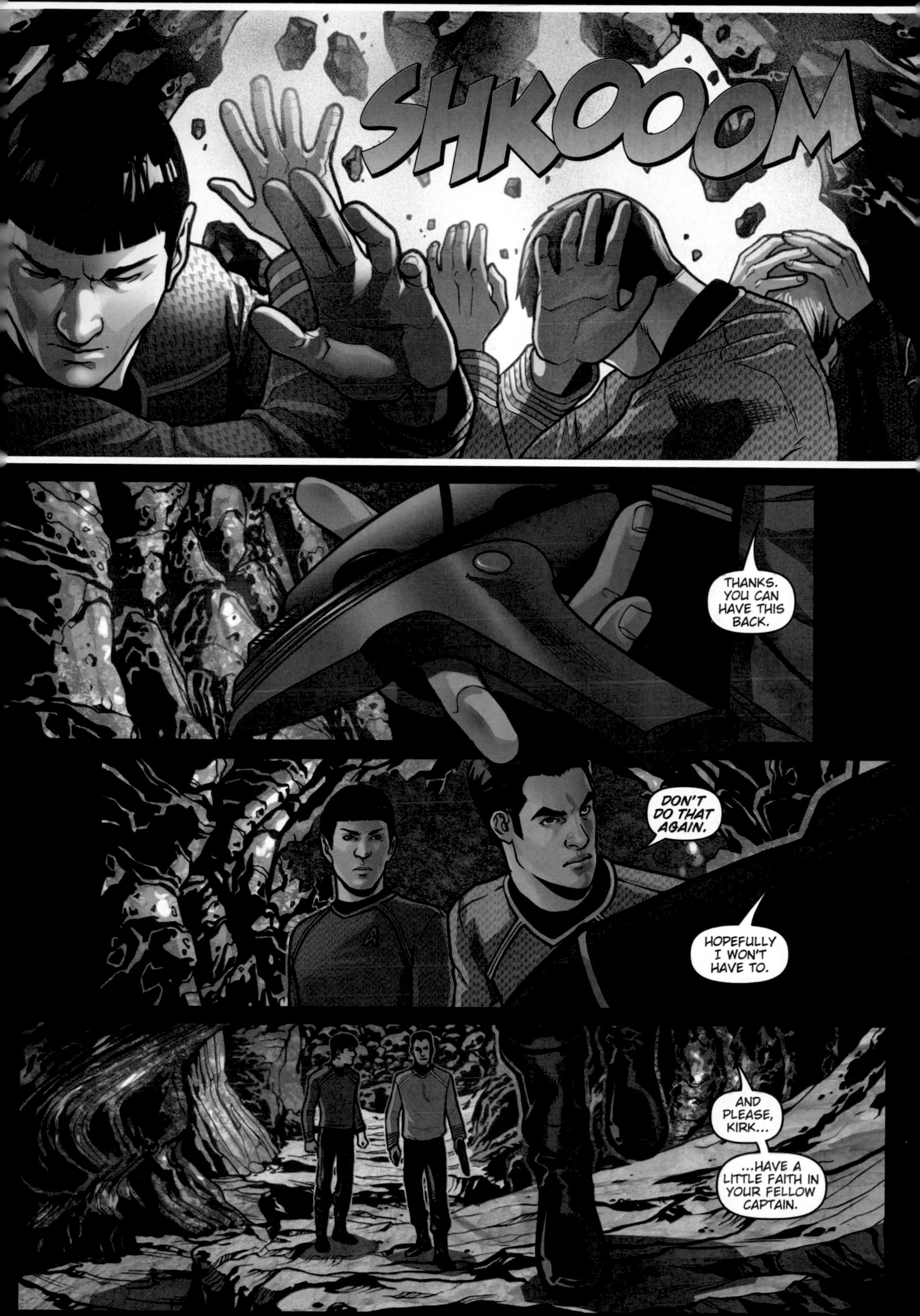
SHKOOOM
THANKS. YOU CAN HAVE THIS BACK.
DON'T DO THAT AGAIN.
HOPEFULLY I WON'T HAVE TO.
AND PLEASE, KIRK...
...HAVE A LITTLE FAITH IN YOUR FELLOW CAPTAIN.

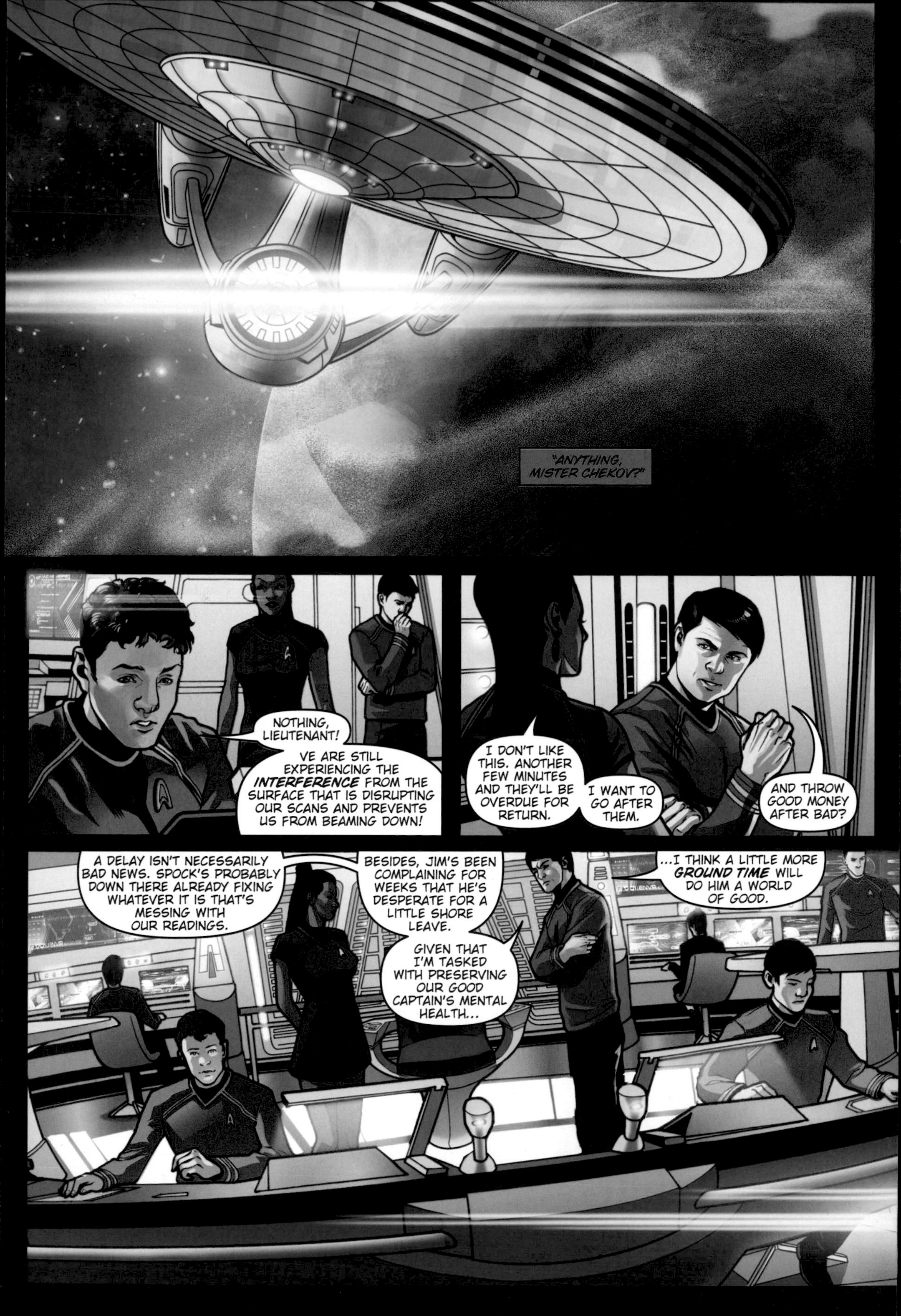
"ANYTHING, MISTER CHEKOV?"
NOTHING, LIEUTENANT!
VE ARE STILL EXPERIENCING THE INTERFERENCE FROM THE SURFACE THAT IS DISRUPTING OUR SCANS AND PREVENTS US FROM BEAMING DOWN!
I DON'T LIKE THIS. ANOTHER FEW MINUTES AND THEY'LL BE OVERDUE FOR RETURN.
I WANT TO GO AFTER THEM.
AND THROW GOOD MONEY AFTER BAD?
A DELAY ISN'T NECESSARILY BAD NEWS. SPOCK'S PROBABLY DOWN THERE ALREADY FIXING WHATEVER IT IS THAT'S MESSING WITH OUR READINGS.
BESIDES, JIM'S BEEN COMPLAINING FOR WEEKS THAT HE'S DESPERATE FOR A LITTLE SHORE LEAVE.
GIVEN THAT I'M TASKED WITH PRESERVING OUR GOOD CAPTAIN'S MENTAL HEALTH...
...I THINK A LITTLE MORE GROUND TIME WILL DO HIM A WORLD OF GOOD.

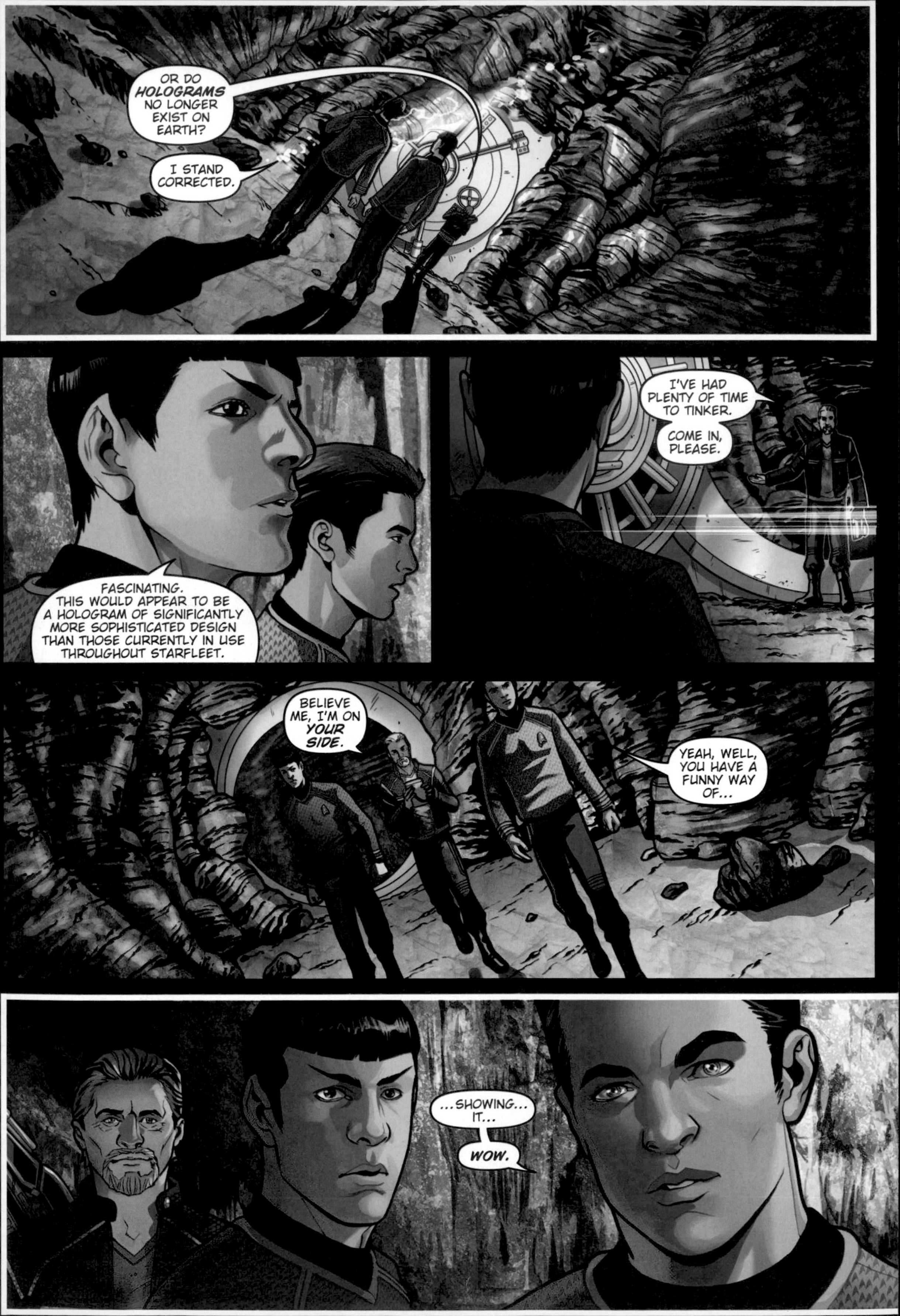
OR DO *HOLOGRAMS* NO LONGER EXIST ON EARTH?
I STAND CORRECTED.
FASCINATING. THIS WOULD APPEAR TO BE A HOLOGRAM OF SIGNIFICANTLY MORE SOPHISTICATED DESIGN THAN THOSE CURRENTLY IN USE THROUGHOUT STARFLEET.
I'VE HAD PLENTY OF TIME TO TINKER.
COME IN, PLEASE.
BELIEVE ME, I'M ON *YOUR SIDE*.
YEAH, WELL, YOU HAVE A FUNNY WAY OF...
...SHOWING... IT...
WOW.

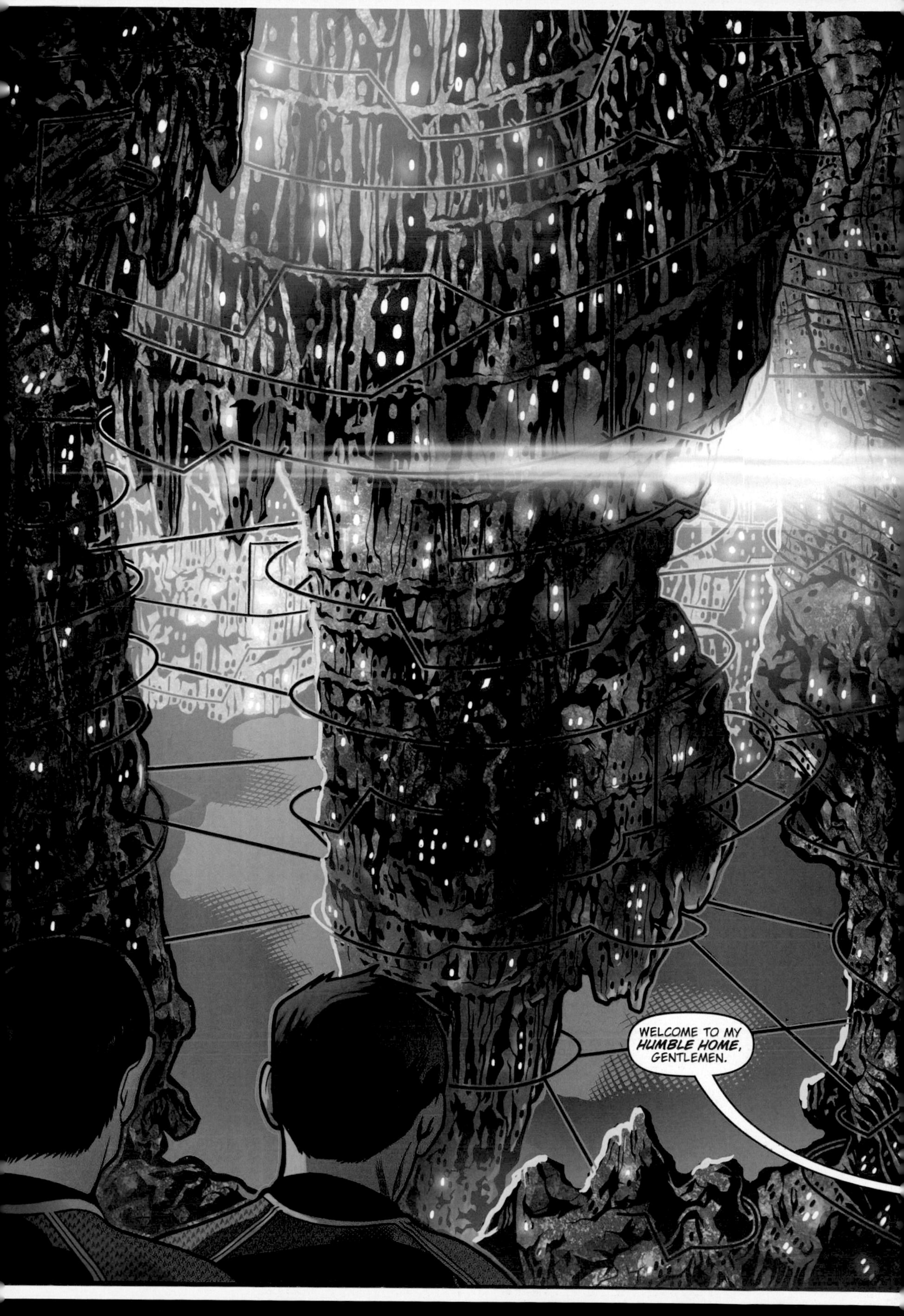
WELCOME TO MY *HUMBLE HOME*, GENTLEMEN.

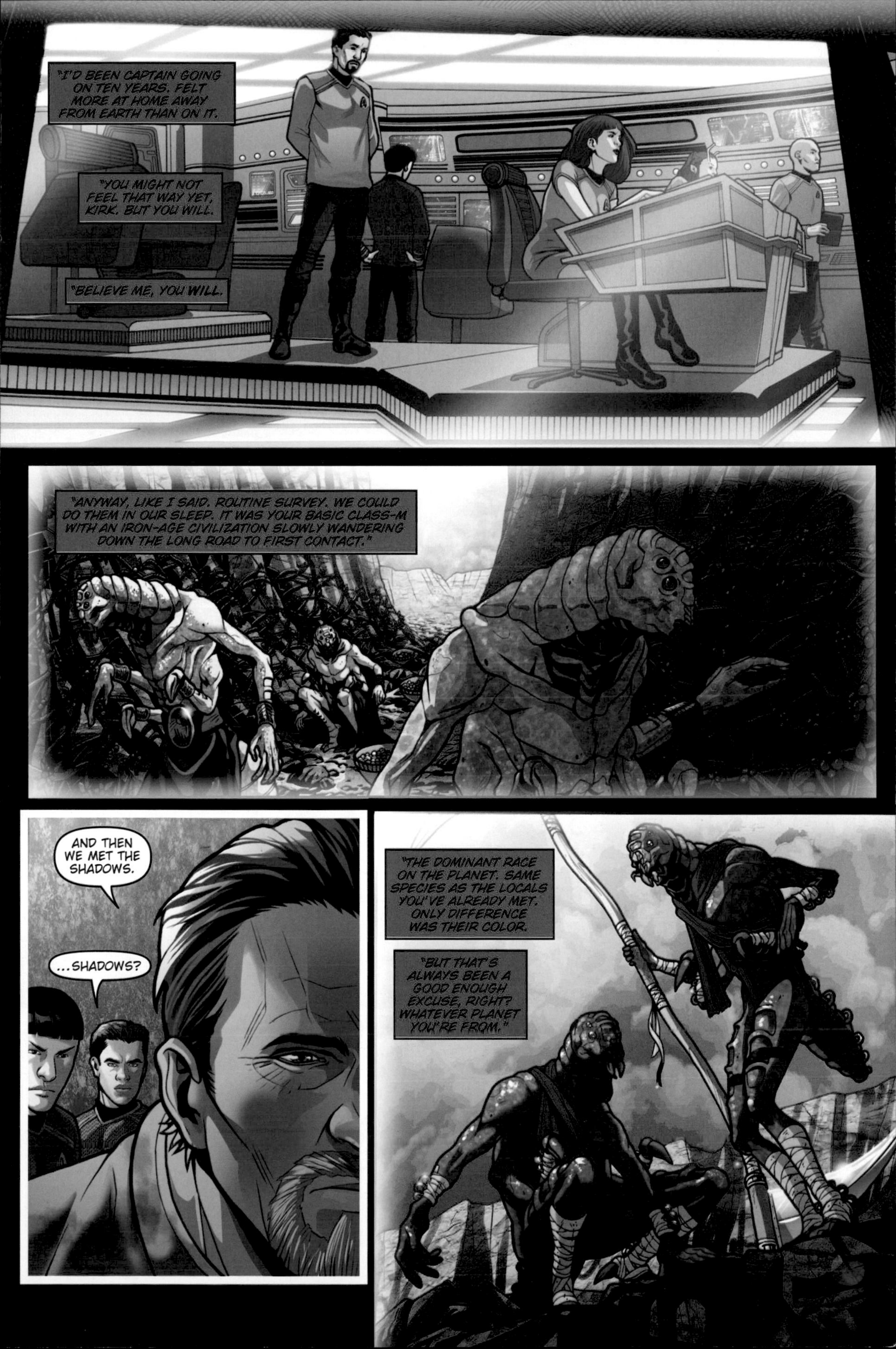
"I'D BEEN CAPTAIN GOING ON TEN YEARS. FELT MORE AT HOME AWAY FROM EARTH THAN ON IT.
"YOU MIGHT NOT FEEL THAT WAY YET, KIRK. BUT YOU WILL.
"BELIEVE ME, YOU WILL.
"ANYWAY, LIKE I SAID. ROUTINE SURVEY. WE COULD DO THEM IN OUR SLEEP. IT WAS YOUR BASIC CLASS-M WITH AN IRON-AGE CIVILIZATION SLOWLY WANDERING DOWN THE LONG ROAD TO FIRST CONTACT."
AND THEN WE MET THE SHADOWS.
...SHADOWS?
"THE DOMINANT RACE ON THE PLANET. SAME SPECIES AS THE LOCALS YOU'VE ALREADY MET. ONLY DIFFERENCE WAS THEIR COLOR.
"BUT THAT'S ALWAYS BEEN A GOOD ENOUGH EXCUSE, RIGHT? WHATEVER PLANET YOU'RE FROM."

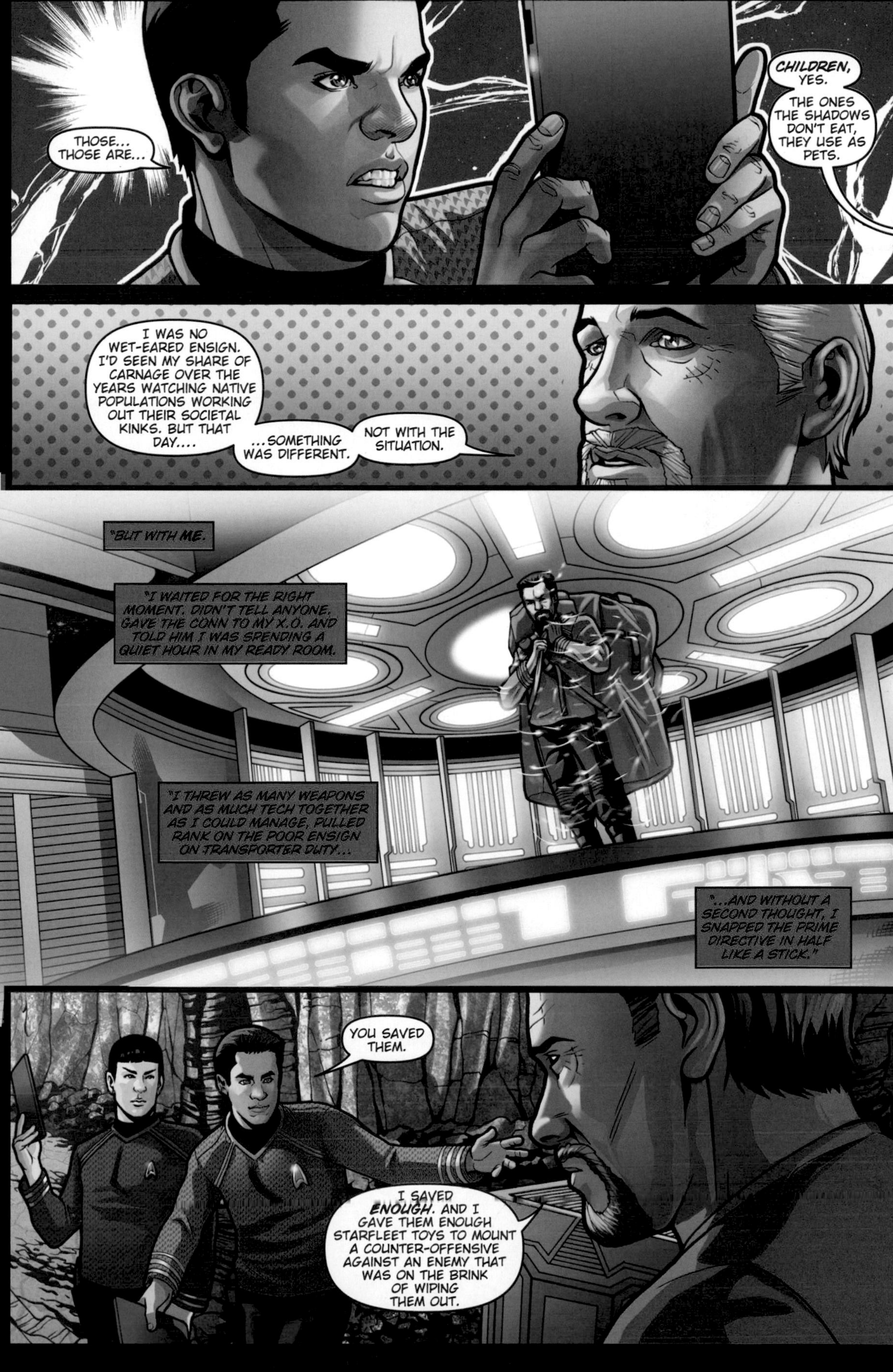
THOSE... THOSE ARE...
CHILDREN, YES.
THE ONES THE SHADOWS DON'T EAT, THEY USE AS PETS.
I WAS NO WET-EARED ENSIGN. I'D SEEN MY SHARE OF CARNAGE OVER THE YEARS WATCHING NATIVE POPULATIONS WORKING OUT THEIR SOCIETAL KINKS. BUT THAT DAY....
...SOMETHING WAS DIFFERENT.
NOT WITH THE SITUATION.
"BUT WITH ME.
"I WAITED FOR THE RIGHT MOMENT. DIDN'T TELL ANYONE. GAVE THE CONN TO MY X.O. AND TOLD HIM I WAS SPENDING A QUIET HOUR IN MY READY ROOM.
"I THREW AS MANY WEAPONS AND AS MUCH TECH TOGETHER AS I COULD MANAGE, PULLED RANK ON THE POOR ENSIGN ON TRANSPORTER DUTY...
"...AND WITHOUT A SECOND THOUGHT, I SNAPPED THE PRIME DIRECTIVE IN HALF LIKE A STICK."
YOU SAVED THEM.
I SAVED ENOUGH. AND I GAVE THEM ENOUGH STARFLEET TOYS TO MOUNT A COUNTER-OFFENSIVE AGAINST AN ENEMY THAT WAS ON THE BRINK OF WIPING THEM OUT.

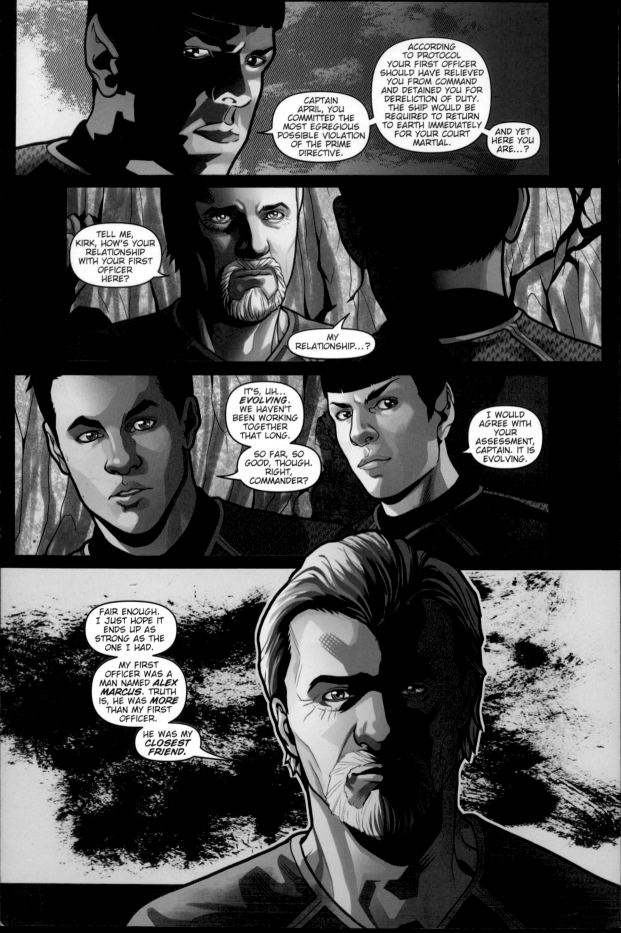

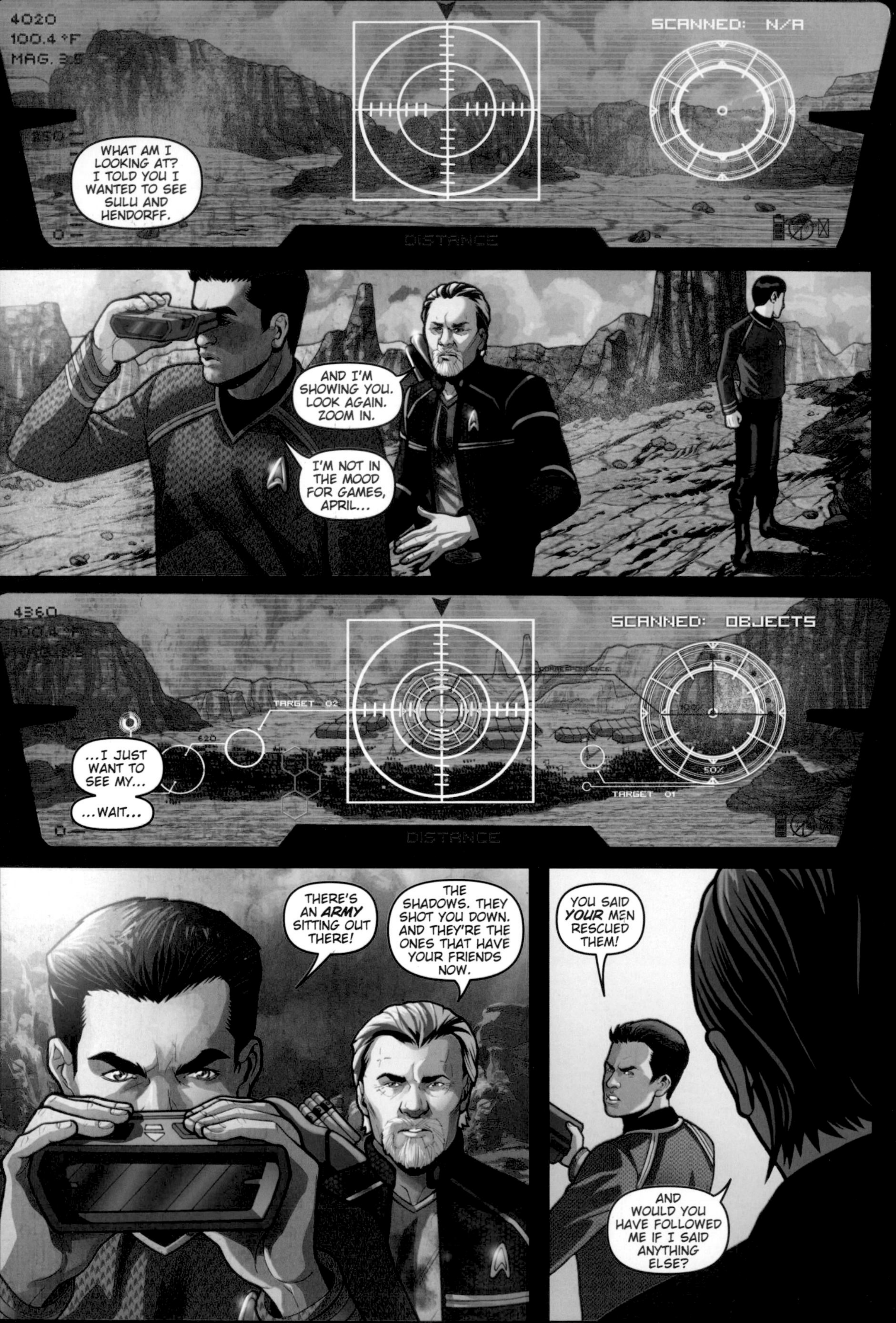
4020
100.4 °F
SCANNED: N/A
WHAT AM I LOOKING AT? I TOLD YOU I WANTED TO SEE SULU AND HENDORFF.
DISTANCE
AND I'M SHOWING YOU. LOOK AGAIN. ZOOM IN.
I'M NOT IN THE MOOD FOR GAMES, APRIL...
4360
SCANNED: OBJECTS
TARGET 02
TARGET 01
...I JUST WANT TO SEE MY...
...WAIT...
DISTANCE
THERE'S AN ARMY SITTING OUT THERE!
THE SHADOWS. THEY SHOT YOU DOWN. AND THEY'RE THE ONES THAT HAVE YOUR FRIENDS NOW.
YOU SAID YOUR MEN RESCUED THEM!
AND WOULD YOU HAVE FOLLOWED ME IF I SAID ANYTHING ELSE?

DAMMIT, APRIL—

"YOUR PEOPLE?" *LISTEN* TO YOURSELF, APRIL! YOU'VE LOST YOUR MIND!

I'M NOT USING THE *ENTERPRISE* TO WIPE OUT AN ARMY *WHO SHOULDN'T EVEN KNOW WE EXIST!*

I NEED YOUR *HELP*, KIRK. THAT ARMY OUT THERE IS THE SHADOWS' *FINAL PUSH* TO WIPE US OUT. SOMEONE'S BEEN SUPPLYING THEM WITH HEAVY *ARTILLERY*. SOMEONE OFF-PLANET, WITH MORE RESOURCES THAN I CAN GET MY HANDS ON.

ALL THAT'S LEFT OF MY PEOPLE ARE HOLED UP IN THESE CAVES. BUT *YOU* CAN SAVE THEM! THE SHADOWS CAN'T WITHSTAND A BOMBARDMENT FROM ORBIT BY A STARSHIP—

SPOKEN LIKE A TRUE BELIEVER IN THE PRIME DIRECTIVE.

BUT *YOU* MADE THE DECISION TO GET IN A SHUTTLE AND COME DOWN HERE, KIRK.

TO COME DOWN HERE JUST LIKE I DID ALL THOSE YEARS AGO. AND, LIKE ME, YOU'RE *INVOLVED NOW.*

SAVE IT, APRIL. I'M GETTING MY MEN BACK—AS *QUICKLY AND QUIETLY* AS POSSIBLE—AND THEN I'M TAKING YOU BACK TO SAN FRANCISCO IN A *HOLDING CELL.*

SPOCK, LET'S GO, WE—

SPOCK...?

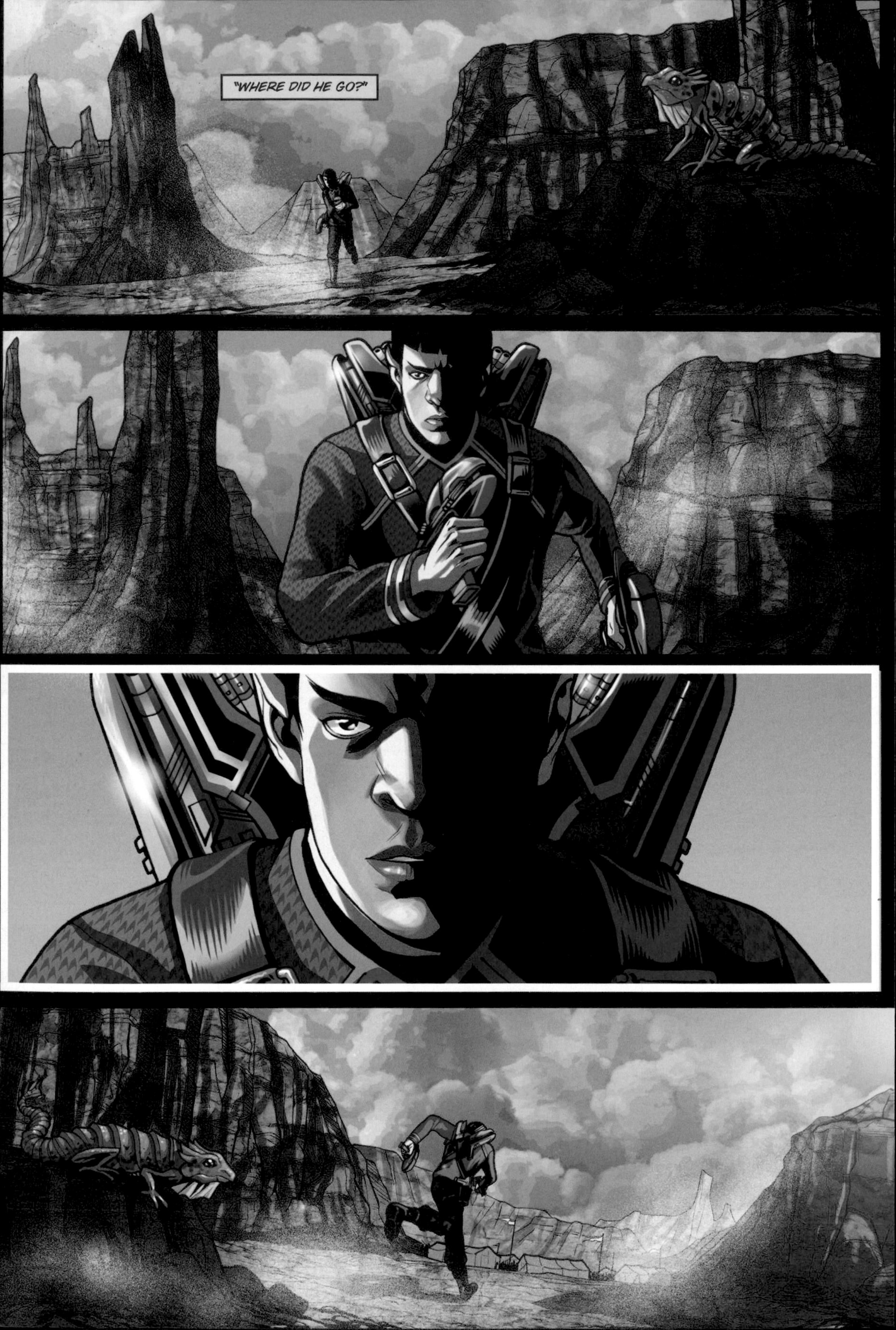
"WHERE DID HE GO?"

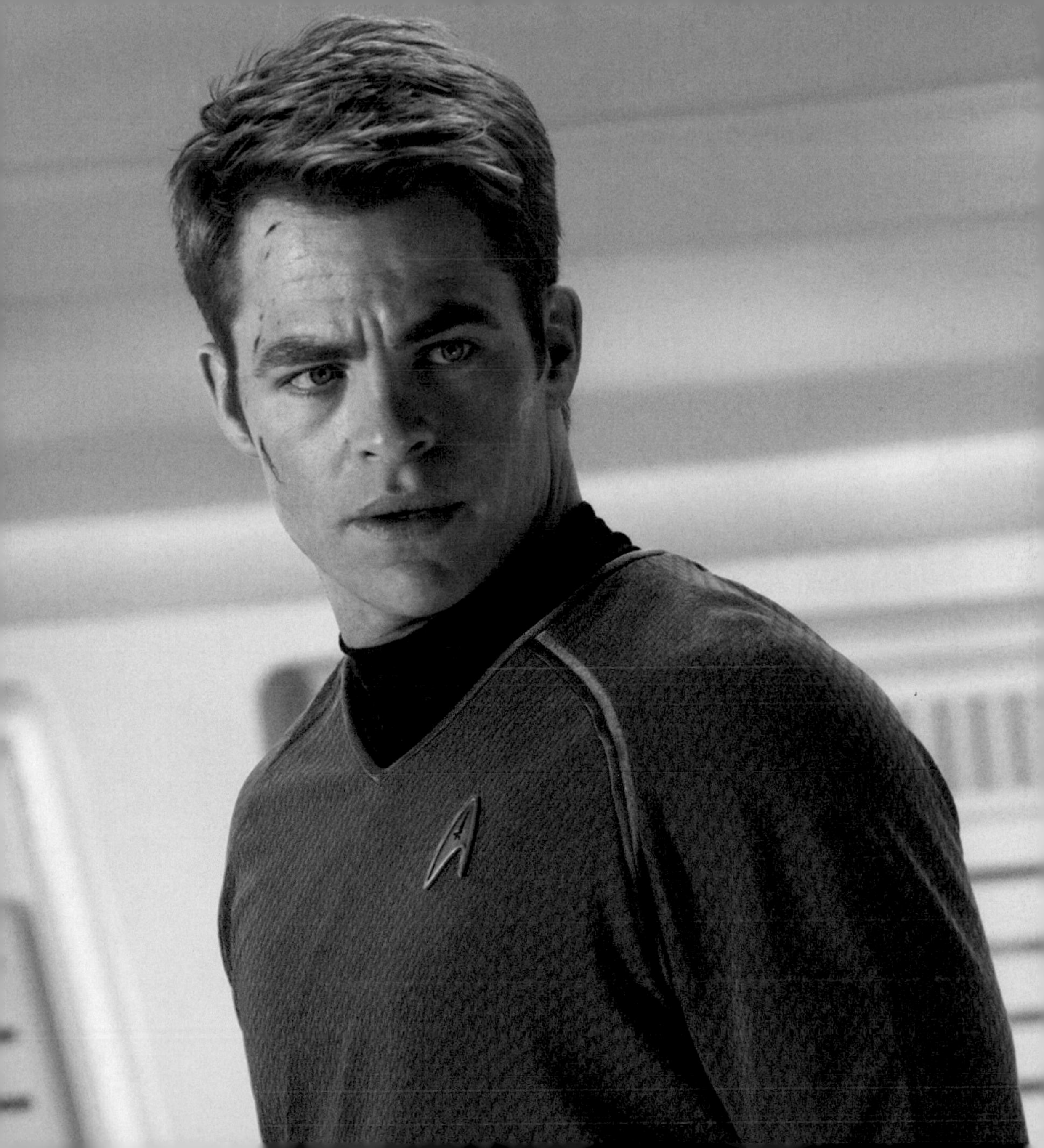

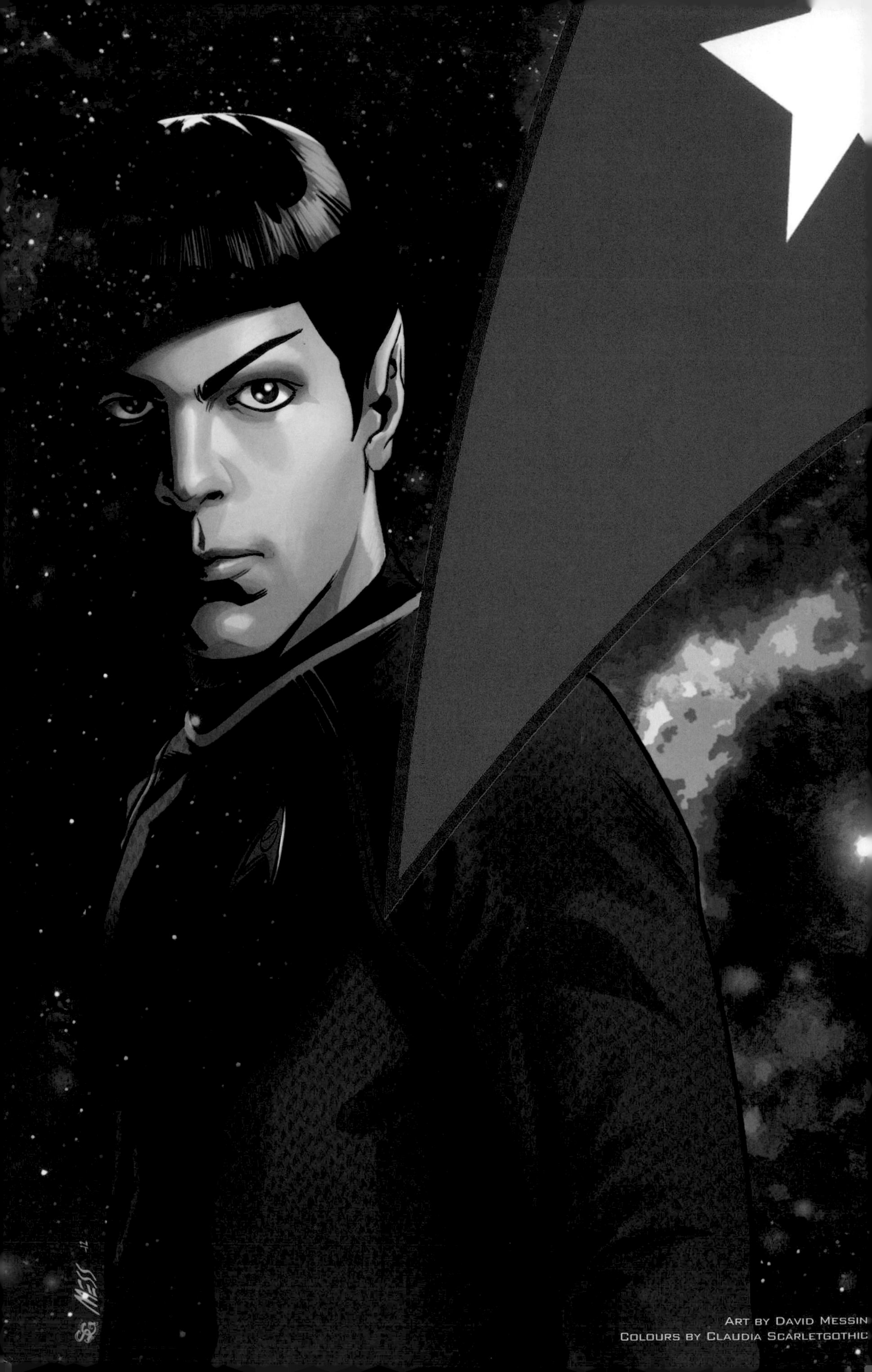

Art by David Messina
Colours by Claudia Scarletgothic

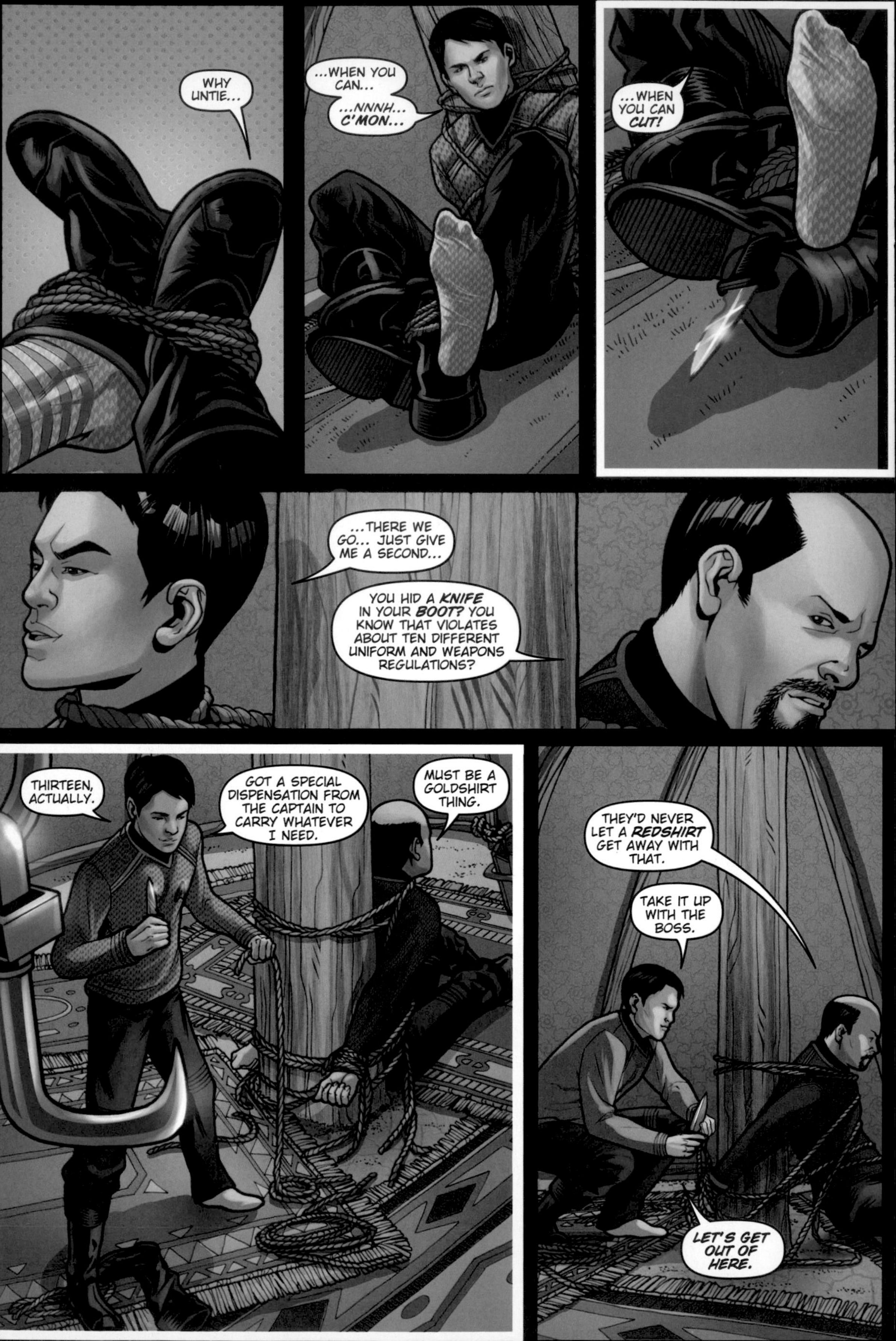
WHY UNTIE...
...WHEN YOU CAN...
...NNNH... C'MON...
...WHEN YOU CAN CUT!
...THERE WE GO... JUST GIVE ME A SECOND...
YOU HID A KNIFE IN YOUR BOOT? YOU KNOW THAT VIOLATES ABOUT TEN DIFFERENT UNIFORM AND WEAPONS REGULATIONS?
THIRTEEN, ACTUALLY.
GOT A SPECIAL DISPENSATION FROM THE CAPTAIN TO CARRY WHATEVER I NEED.
MUST BE A GOLDSHIRT THING.
THEY'D NEVER LET A REDSHIRT GET AWAY WITH THAT.
TAKE IT UP WITH THE BOSS.
LET'S GET OUT OF HERE.

I'M GOING AFTER SPOCK. DON'T TRY TO STOP ME, APRIL.

YOU'RE JUST THROWING GOOD MONEY AFTER BAD, CAPTAIN.

I'M NOT ASKING FOR YOUR *ADVICE!* YOU SHOULDN'T HAVE LIED TO ME ABOUT SULLU AND HENDORFF BEING SAFE IN YOUR HANDS!

I MADE A *TACTICAL DECISION.* I NEED YOUR *HELP*, KIRK. I'M FIGHTING TO PROTECT A PEOPLE ON THE VERGE OF BEING *WIPED OUT.* IF I HAD TOLD YOU WHERE YOUR MEN WERE, YOU MIGHT HAVE RUSHED OFF AND GOTTEN YOURSELF KILLED.

JUST LIKE YOU'RE DOING NOW.

CH'K TAK TIL CHOK TA

GOOD. I'LL BE RIGHT THERE.

WHAT'S GOING ON?

A NEW ARRIVAL.

YOU MIGHT WANT TO POSTPONE YOUR RESCUE.

RRRRVVVVMMM

YOU TOOK YOUR SWEET TIME.

DID YOU GET EVERYTHING I ASKED FOR?

YOU MUST BE KIRK. WORD GETS AROUND. HERO OF THE FEDERATION. YOUNGEST CAPTAIN IN THE FLEET.

I'M *MUDD*. AND I'M SINGLE, JUST SO YOU KNOW.

AND MORE. BUT IT'S GONNA BE EXPENSIVE FOR YOU, BOBBY. IT'S GETTING HARDER TO FIND THE AMMO YOU'RE LOOKING FOR, NOT TO MENTION SMUGGLING IT ACROSS THE QUADRANT.

WORSE NEWS? IT'S ALL IN MY SHUTTLE, WHICH IS CURRENTLY A PRISONER IN A HANGAR ON THE *ENTERPRISE*. SOMETHING ABOUT VIOLATING A FANCY DIRECTIVE...

...TOOK ALL MY CHARM JUST TO CONVINCE THEM TO BRING ME DOWN HERE.

THAT'S ENOUGH, MUDD.

CAPTAIN, WHAT HAPPENED?

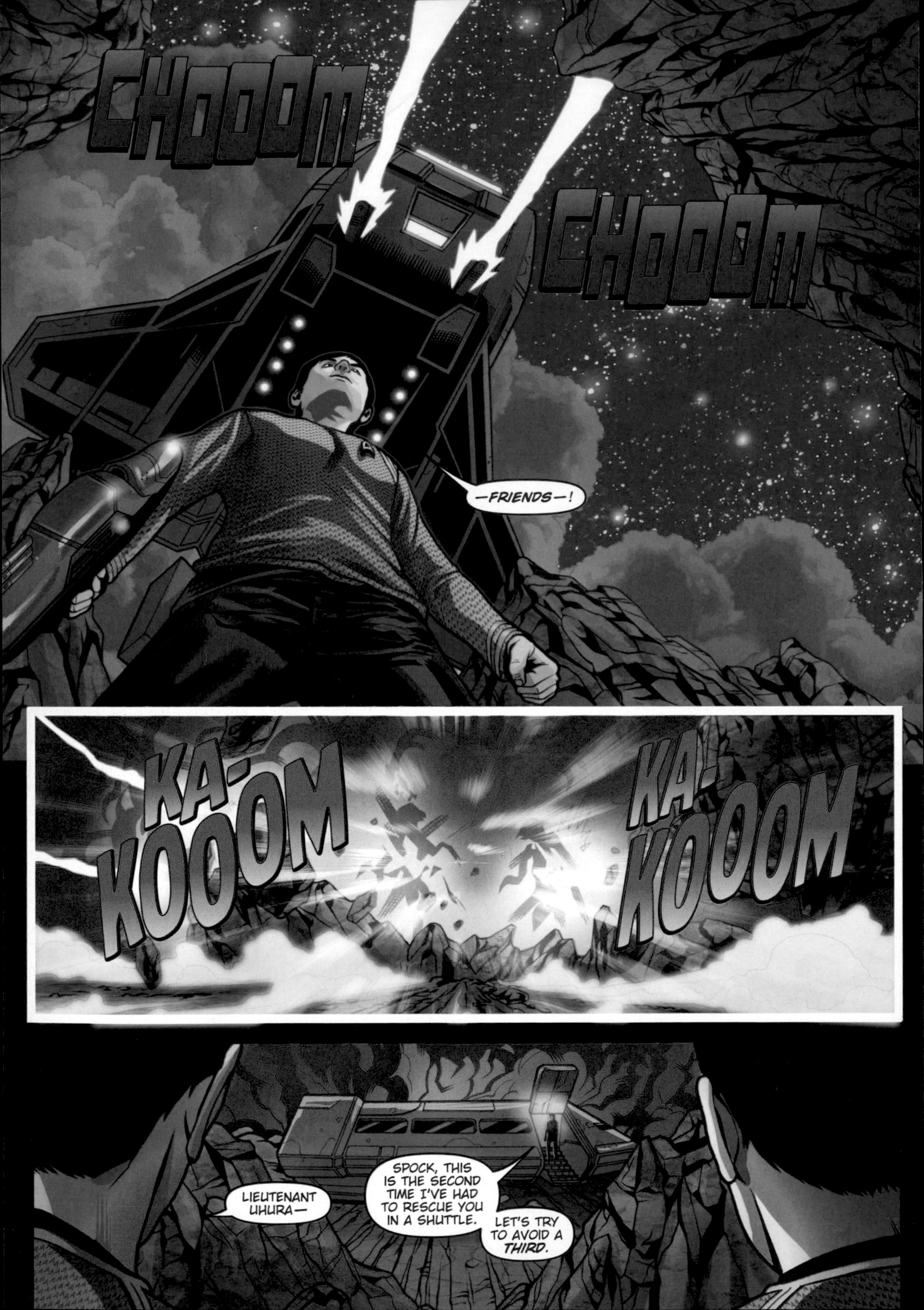
CHOOOM
CHOOOM
—FRIENDS—!
KA-KOOOM
KA-KOOOM
SPOCK, THIS IS THE SECOND TIME I'VE HAD TO RESCUE YOU IN A SHUTTLE.
LIEUTENANT UHURA—
LET'S TRY TO AVOID A *THIRD*.

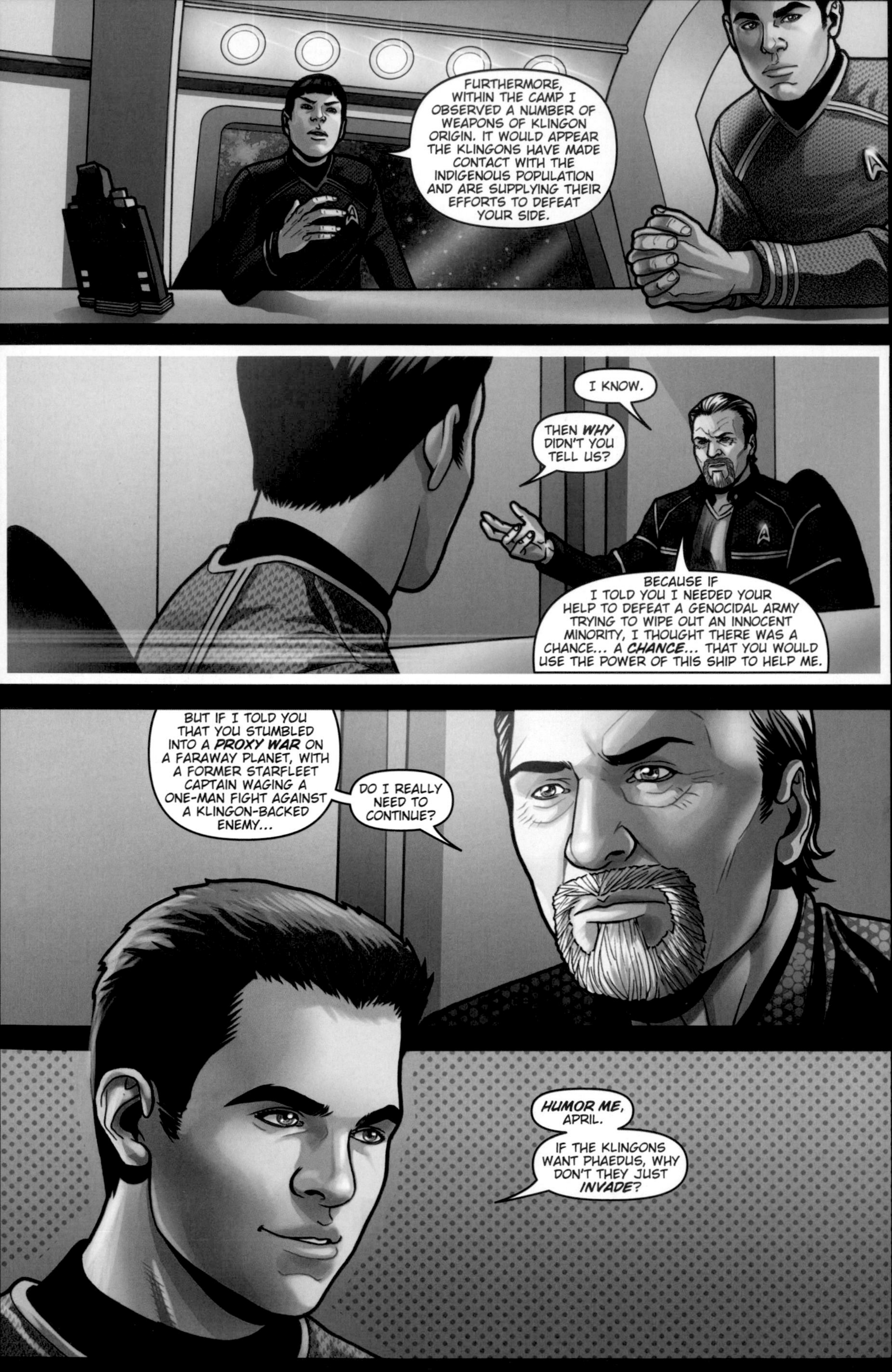
FURTHERMORE, WITHIN THE CAMP I OBSERVED A NUMBER OF WEAPONS OF KLINGON ORIGIN. IT WOULD APPEAR THE KLINGONS HAVE MADE CONTACT WITH THE INDIGENOUS POPULATION AND ARE SUPPLYING THEIR EFFORTS TO DEFEAT YOUR SIDE.
I KNOW.
THEN WHY DIDN'T YOU TELL US?
BECAUSE IF I TOLD YOU I NEEDED YOUR HELP TO DEFEAT A GENOCIDAL ARMY TRYING TO WIPE OUT AN INNOCENT MINORITY, I THOUGHT THERE WAS A CHANCE... A CHANCE... THAT YOU WOULD USE THE POWER OF THIS SHIP TO HELP ME.
BUT IF I TOLD YOU THAT YOU STUMBLED INTO A PROXY WAR ON A FARAWAY PLANET, WITH A FORMER STARFLEET CAPTAIN WAGING A ONE-MAN FIGHT AGAINST A KLINGON-BACKED ENEMY...
DO I REALLY NEED TO CONTINUE?
HUMOR ME, APRIL.
IF THE KLINGONS WANT PHAEDUS, WHY DON'T THEY JUST INVADE?

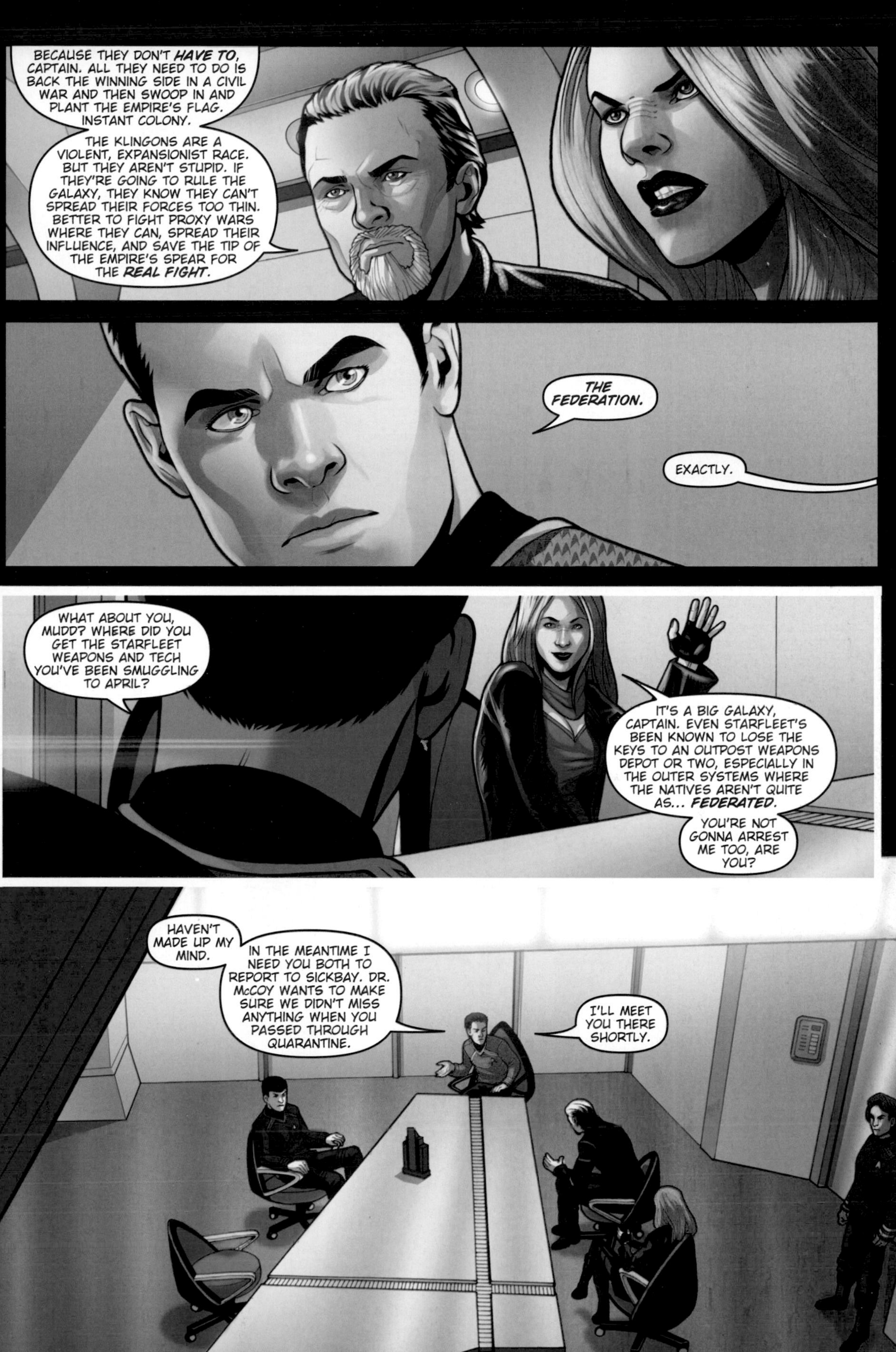
BECAUSE THEY DON'T HAVE TO, CAPTAIN. ALL THEY NEED TO DO IS BACK THE WINNING SIDE IN A CIVIL WAR AND THEN SWOOP IN AND PLANT THE EMPIRE'S FLAG. INSTANT COLONY.
THE KLINGONS ARE A VIOLENT, EXPANSIONIST RACE. BUT THEY AREN'T STUPID. IF THEY'RE GOING TO RULE THE GALAXY, THEY KNOW THEY CAN'T SPREAD THEIR FORCES TOO THIN. BETTER TO FIGHT PROXY WARS WHERE THEY CAN, SPREAD THEIR INFLUENCE, AND SAVE THE TIP OF THE EMPIRE'S SPEAR FOR THE REAL FIGHT.
THE FEDERATION.
EXACTLY.
WHAT ABOUT YOU, MUDD? WHERE DID YOU GET THE STARFLEET WEAPONS AND TECH YOU'VE BEEN SMUGGLING TO APRIL?
IT'S A BIG GALAXY, CAPTAIN. EVEN STARFLEET'S BEEN KNOWN TO LOSE THE KEYS TO AN OUTPOST WEAPONS DEPOT OR TWO, ESPECIALLY IN THE OUTER SYSTEMS WHERE THE NATIVES AREN'T QUITE AS... FEDERATED.
YOU'RE NOT GONNA ARREST ME TOO, ARE YOU?
HAVEN'T MADE UP MY MIND.
IN THE MEANTIME I NEED YOU BOTH TO REPORT TO SICKBAY. DR. McCOY WANTS TO MAKE SURE WE DIDN'T MISS ANYTHING WHEN YOU PASSED THROUGH QUARANTINE.
I'LL MEET YOU THERE SHORTLY.

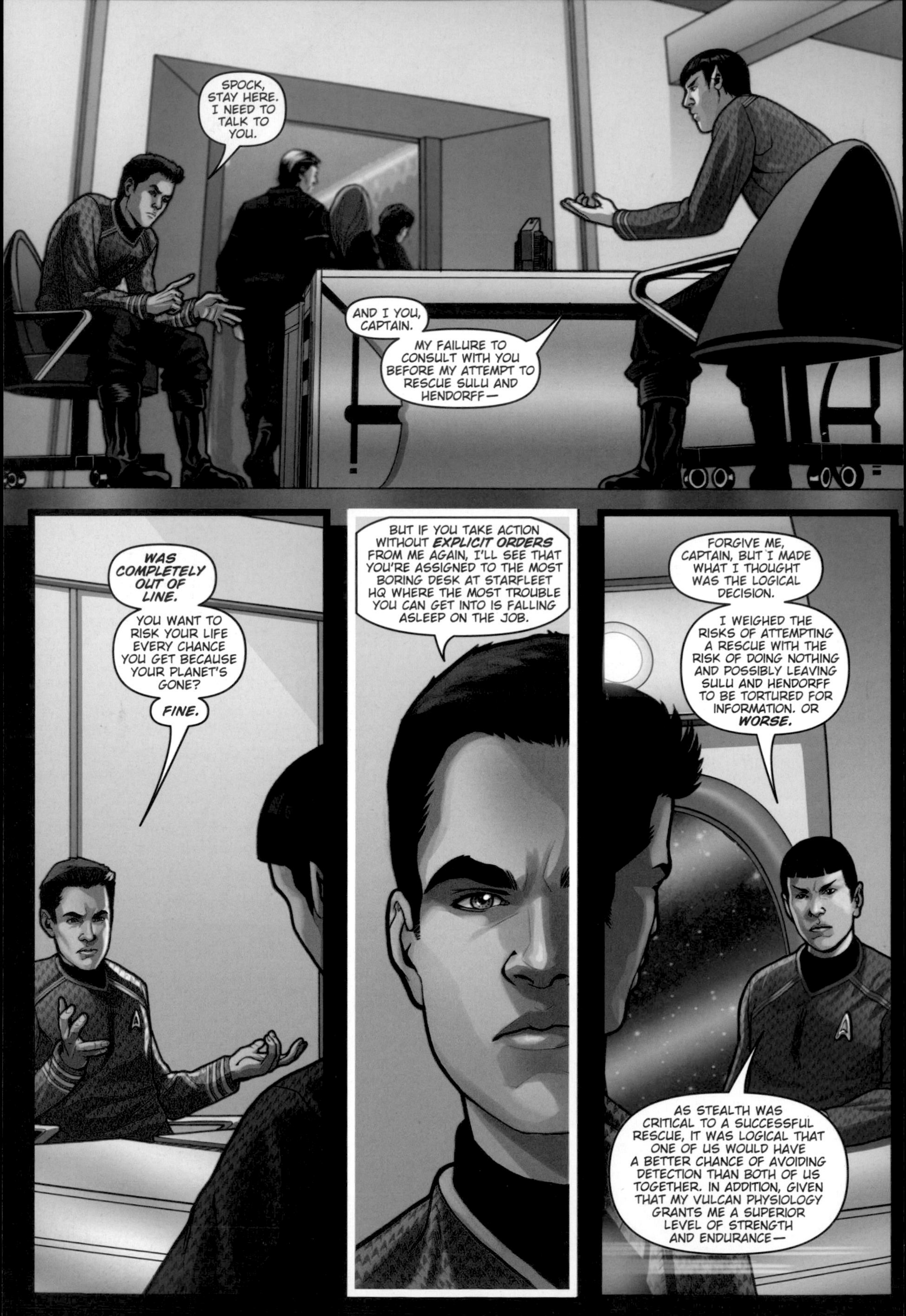
SPOCK, STAY HERE. I NEED TO TALK TO YOU.
AND I YOU, CAPTAIN.
MY FAILURE TO CONSULT WITH YOU BEFORE MY ATTEMPT TO RESCUE SULU AND HENDORFF—
WAS COMPLETELY OUT OF LINE.
YOU WANT TO RISK YOUR LIFE EVERY CHANCE YOU GET BECAUSE YOUR PLANET'S GONE?
FINE.
BUT IF YOU TAKE ACTION WITHOUT EXPLICIT ORDERS FROM ME AGAIN, I'LL SEE THAT YOU'RE ASSIGNED TO THE MOST BORING DESK AT STARFLEET HQ WHERE THE MOST TROUBLE YOU CAN GET INTO IS FALLING ASLEEP ON THE JOB.
FORGIVE ME, CAPTAIN, BUT I MADE WHAT I THOUGHT WAS THE LOGICAL DECISION.
I WEIGHED THE RISKS OF ATTEMPTING A RESCUE WITH THE RISK OF DOING NOTHING AND POSSIBLY LEAVING SULU AND HENDORFF TO BE TORTURED FOR INFORMATION. OR WORSE.
AS STEALTH WAS CRITICAL TO A SUCCESSFUL RESCUE, IT WAS LOGICAL THAT ONE OF US WOULD HAVE A BETTER CHANCE OF AVOIDING DETECTION THAN BOTH OF US TOGETHER. IN ADDITION, GIVEN THAT MY VULCAN PHYSIOLOGY GRANTS ME A SUPERIOR LEVEL OF STRENGTH AND ENDURANCE—

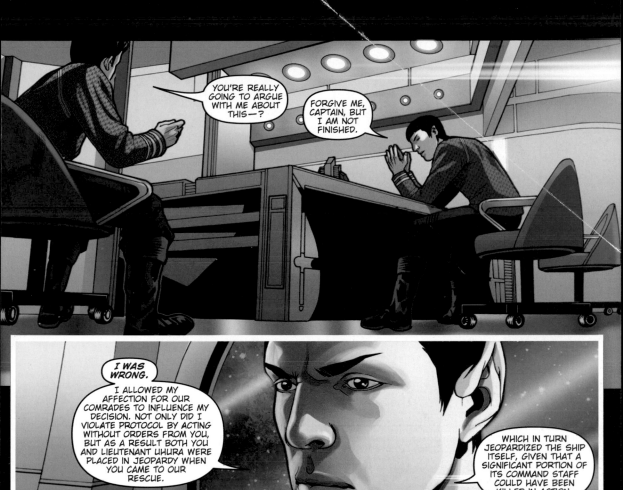

YOU'RE REALLY GOING TO ARGUE WITH ME ABOUT THIS—?

FORGIVE ME, CAPTAIN, BUT I AM NOT FINISHED.

I WAS WRONG.

I ALLOWED MY AFFECTION FOR OUR COMRADES TO INFLUENCE MY DECISION. NOT ONLY DID I VIOLATE PROTOCOL BY ACTING WITHOUT ORDERS FROM YOU, BUT AS A RESULT BOTH YOU AND LIEUTENANT UHURA WERE PLACED IN JEOPARDY WHEN YOU CAME TO OUR RESCUE.

WHICH IN TURN JEOPARDIZED THE SHIP ITSELF, GIVEN THAT A SIGNIFICANT PORTION OF ITS COMMAND STAFF COULD HAVE BEEN KILLED IN ACTION.

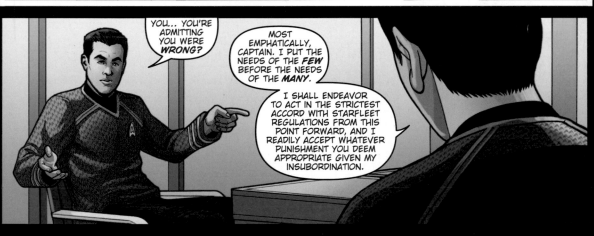

YOU... YOU'RE ADMITTING YOU WERE WRONG?

MOST EMPHATICALLY, CAPTAIN. I PUT THE NEEDS OF THE FEW BEFORE THE NEEDS OF THE MANY.

I SHALL ENDEAVOR TO ACT IN THE STRICTEST ACCORD WITH STARFLEET REGULATIONS FROM THIS POINT FORWARD, AND I READILY ACCEPT WHATEVER PUNISHMENT YOU DEEM APPROPRIATE GIVEN MY INSUBORDINATION.

PUNISHMENT?

I'M JUST GLAD YOU'RE NOT DEAD, SPOCK.

BESIDES, YOU STILL HAVE TO ANSWER TO LIEUTENANT UHURA...

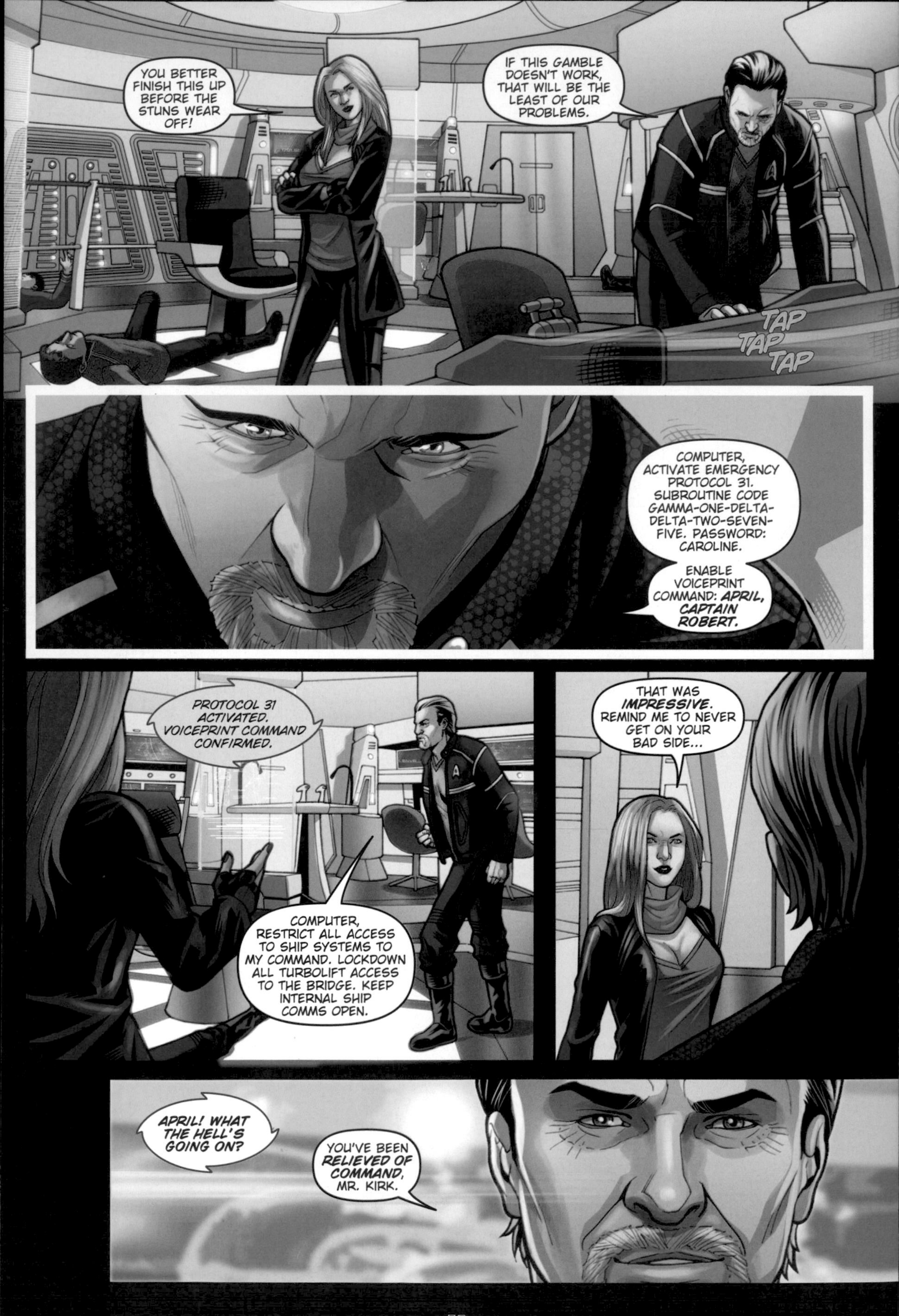
YOU BETTER FINISH THIS UP BEFORE THE STUNS WEAR OFF!
IF THIS GAMBLE DOESN'T WORK, THAT WILL BE THE LEAST OF OUR PROBLEMS.
TAP TAP TAP
COMPUTER, ACTIVATE EMERGENCY PROTOCOL 31. SUBROUTINE CODE GAMMA-ONE-DELTA-DELTA-TWO-SEVEN-FIVE. PASSWORD: CAROLINE.
ENABLE VOICEPRINT COMMAND: **APRIL, CAPTAIN ROBERT.**
PROTOCOL 31 ACTIVATED. VOICEPRINT COMMAND CONFIRMED.
COMPUTER, RESTRICT ALL ACCESS TO SHIP SYSTEMS TO MY COMMAND. LOCKDOWN ALL TURBOLIFT ACCESS TO THE BRIDGE. KEEP INTERNAL SHIP COMMS OPEN.
THAT WAS ***IMPRESSIVE***. REMIND ME TO NEVER GET ON YOUR BAD SIDE...
APRIL! WHAT THE HELL'S GOING ON?
YOU'VE BEEN ***RELIEVED OF COMMAND***, MR. KIRK.

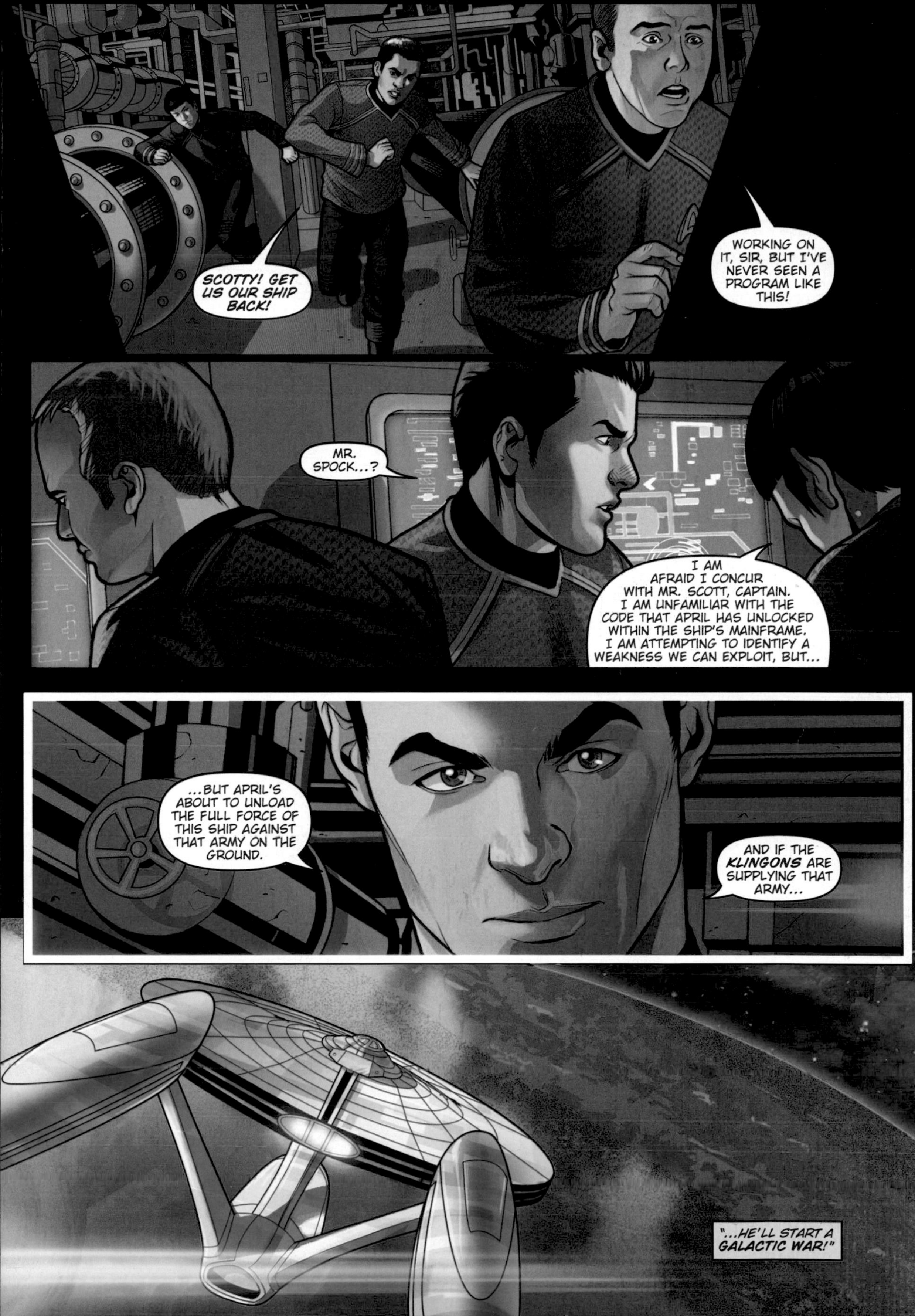
SCOTTY! GET US OUR SHIP BACK!
WORKING ON IT, SIR, BUT I'VE NEVER SEEN A PROGRAM LIKE THIS!
MR. SPOCK...?
I AM AFRAID I CONCUR WITH MR. SCOTT, CAPTAIN. I AM UNFAMILIAR WITH THE CODE THAT APRIL HAS UNLOCKED WITHIN THE SHIP'S MAINFRAME. I AM ATTEMPTING TO IDENTIFY A WEAKNESS WE CAN EXPLOIT, BUT...
...BUT APRIL'S ABOUT TO UNLOAD THE FULL FORCE OF THIS SHIP AGAINST THAT ARMY ON THE GROUND.
AND IF THE KLINGONS ARE SUPPLYING THAT ARMY...
"...HE'LL START A GALACTIC WAR!"

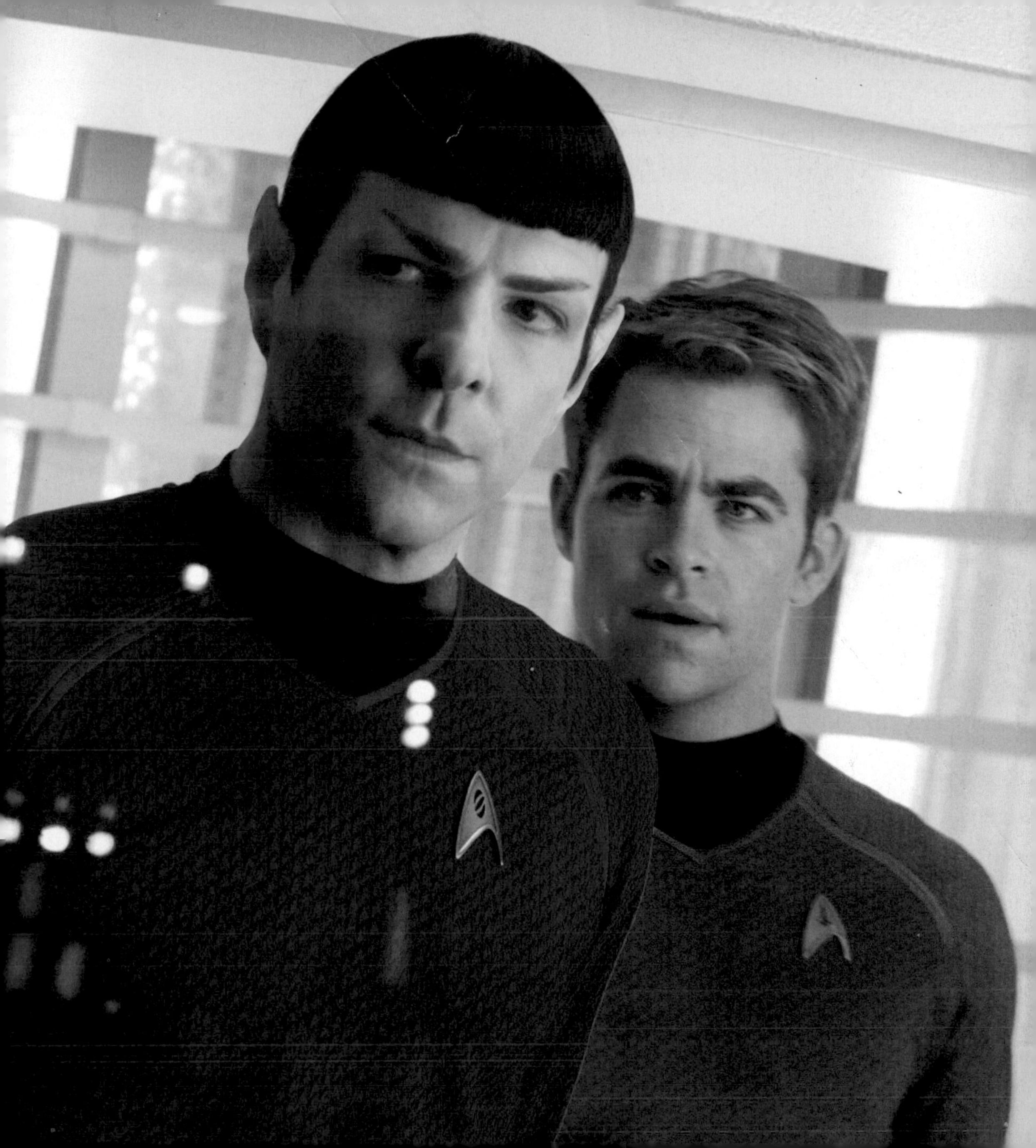

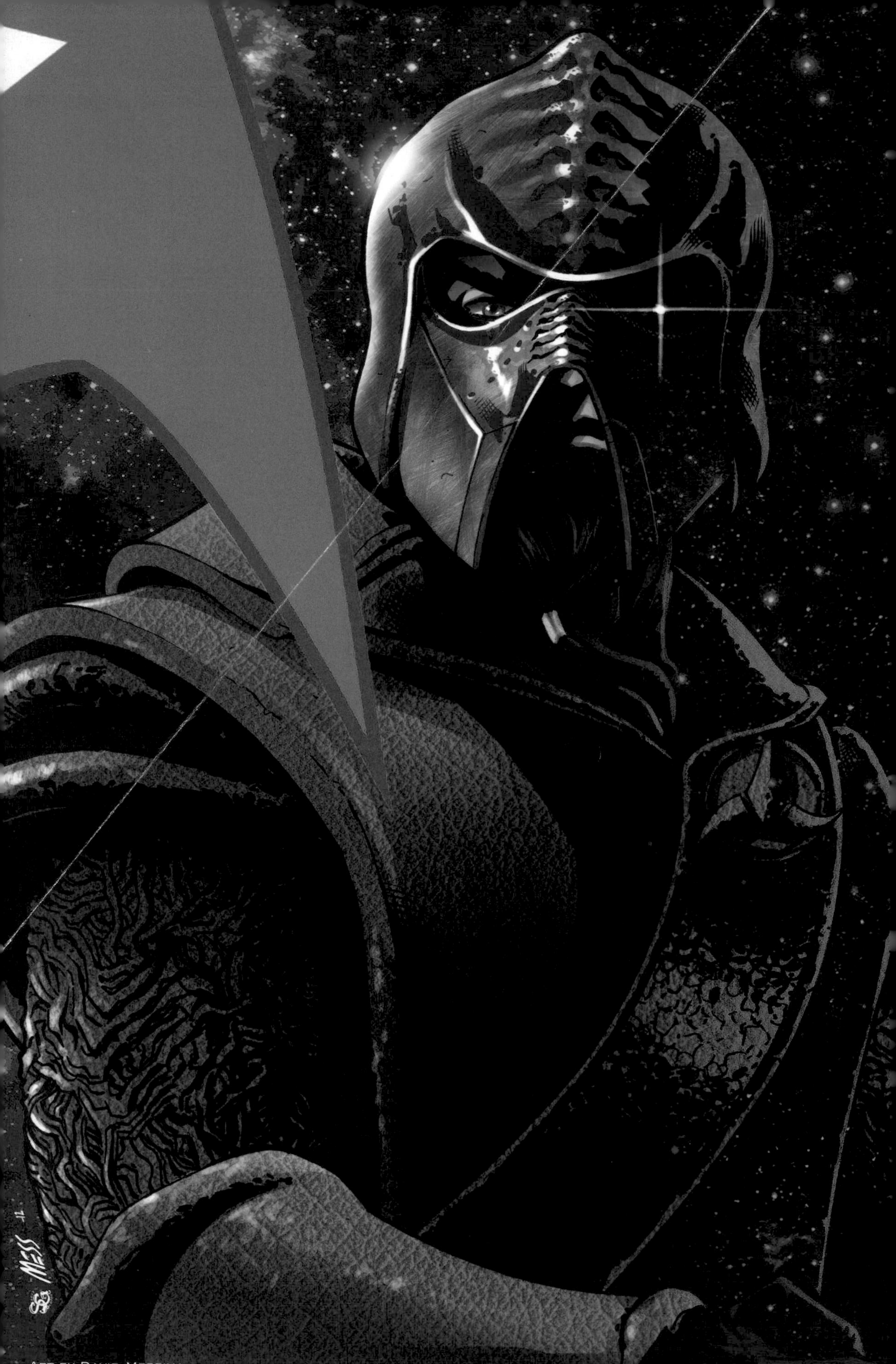
MESS '12

Art by David Messina
Colours by Claudia Scarletgothica

"HOW DO WE GET OUR
SHIP BACK, SCOTTY?"

"WELL, SIR, THE GOOD NEWS IS THAT THE
UNEXPECTED ARRIVAL OF YOUR SHIP ARRIVED
[UNREADABLE] COME TO FIGHT, IT WAS
[UNREADABLE] A WAY TO GET OUR ATTENTION."

BUT THE *CATASTROPHIC* NEWS IS
THAT WHATEVER PROGRAM APRIL
ACTIVATED INSIDE THE SHIP'S
COMPUTER HAS LOCKED US
OUT OF EVERYTHING! HE
CONTROLS IT ALL FROM
THE BRIDGE NOW!

THEN WE
TAKE THE
BRIDGE.

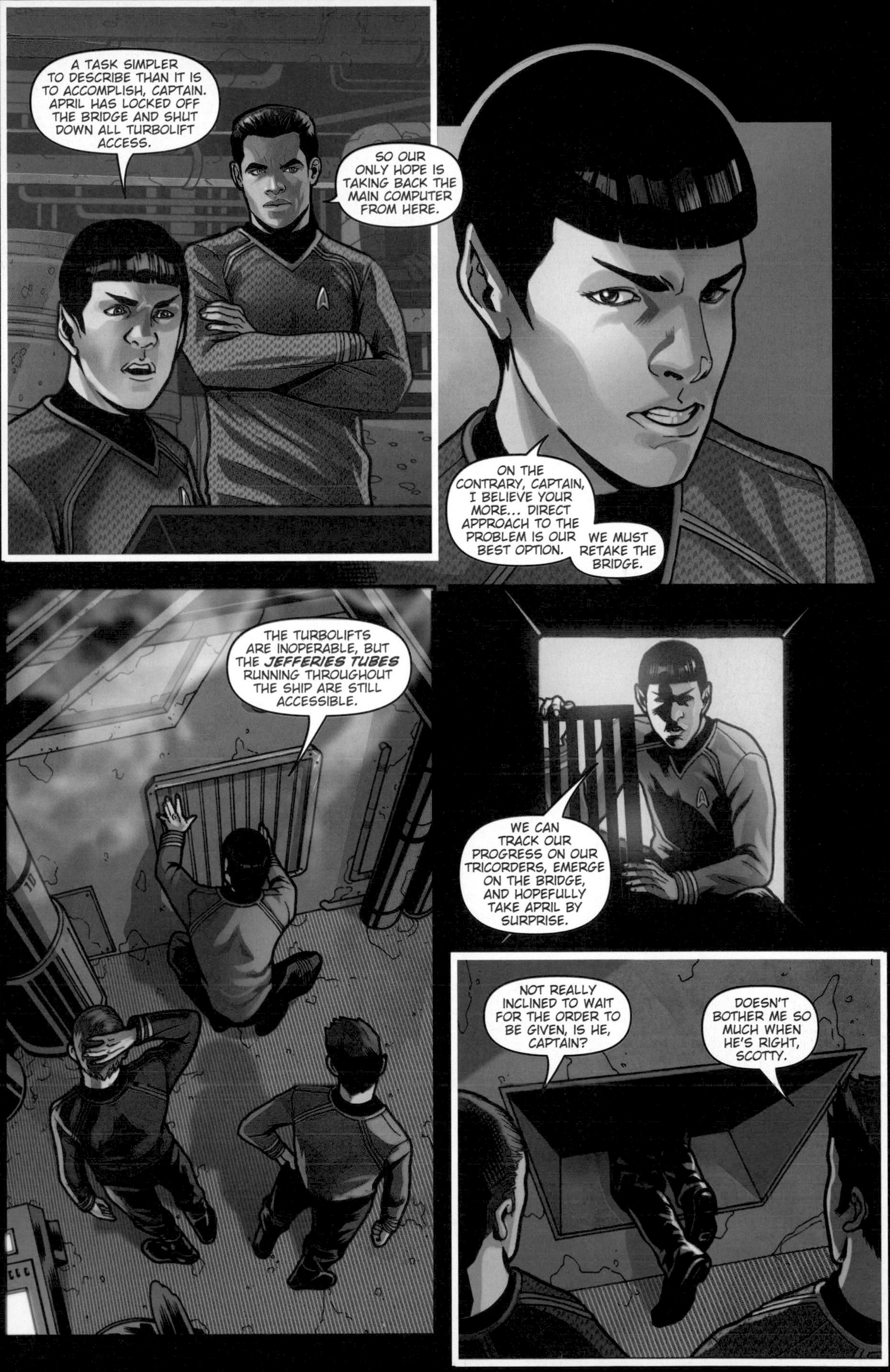
A TASK SIMPLER TO DESCRIBE THAN IT IS TO ACCOMPLISH, CAPTAIN. APRIL HAS LOCKED OFF THE BRIDGE AND SHUT DOWN ALL TURBOLIFT ACCESS.
SO OUR ONLY HOPE IS TAKING BACK THE MAIN COMPUTER FROM HERE.
ON THE CONTRARY, CAPTAIN, I BELIEVE YOUR MORE... DIRECT APPROACH TO THE PROBLEM IS OUR BEST OPTION.
WE MUST RETAKE THE BRIDGE.
THE TURBOLIFTS ARE INOPERABLE, BUT THE *JEFFERIES TUBES* RUNNING THROUGHOUT THE SHIP ARE STILL ACCESSIBLE.
WE CAN TRACK OUR PROGRESS ON OUR TRICORDERS, EMERGE ON THE BRIDGE, AND HOPEFULLY TAKE APRIL BY SURPRISE.
NOT REALLY INCLINED TO WAIT FOR THE ORDER TO BE GIVEN, IS HE, CAPTAIN?
DOESN'T BOTHER ME SO MUCH WHEN HE'S RIGHT, SCOTTY.

I WOULD DO EXACTLY THE SAME THING IN YOUR POSITION, OF COURSE.

THE BACKDOOR PROGRAM I'VE ACTIVATED IN THE *ENTERPRISE* MAINFRAME CAN'T BE STOPPED FROM ANYWHERE BUT WHERE I STAND NOW.

A PHYSICAL ASSAULT ON THE BRIDGE IS NOT JUST YOUR BEST OPTION...

...IT'S YOUR *ONLY* ONE.

BUT CONTROL OF THE SHIP'S SYSTEMS MEANS *ALL SYSTEMS.*

INCLUDING THE TUBES.

RRRRNNNN

SPOCK!

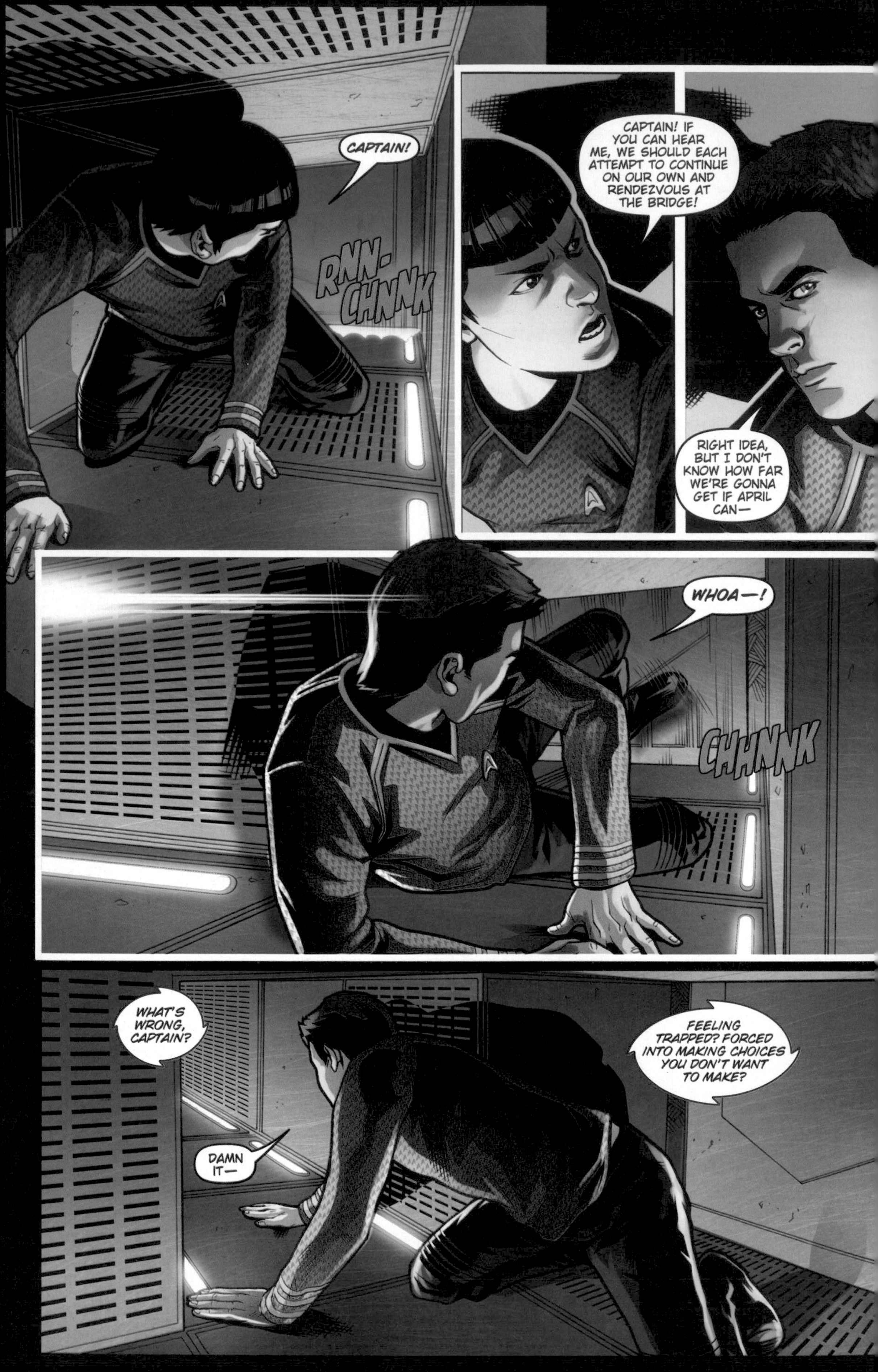
CAPTAIN!
RNN-CHNNK
CAPTAIN! IF YOU CAN HEAR ME, WE SHOULD EACH ATTEMPT TO CONTINUE ON OUR OWN AND RENDEZVOUS AT THE BRIDGE!
RIGHT IDEA, BUT I DON'T KNOW HOW FAR WE'RE GONNA GET IF APRIL CAN—
WHOA—!
CHHNNK
WHAT'S WRONG, CAPTAIN?
FEELING TRAPPED? FORCED INTO MAKING CHOICES YOU DON'T WANT TO MAKE?
DAMN IT—

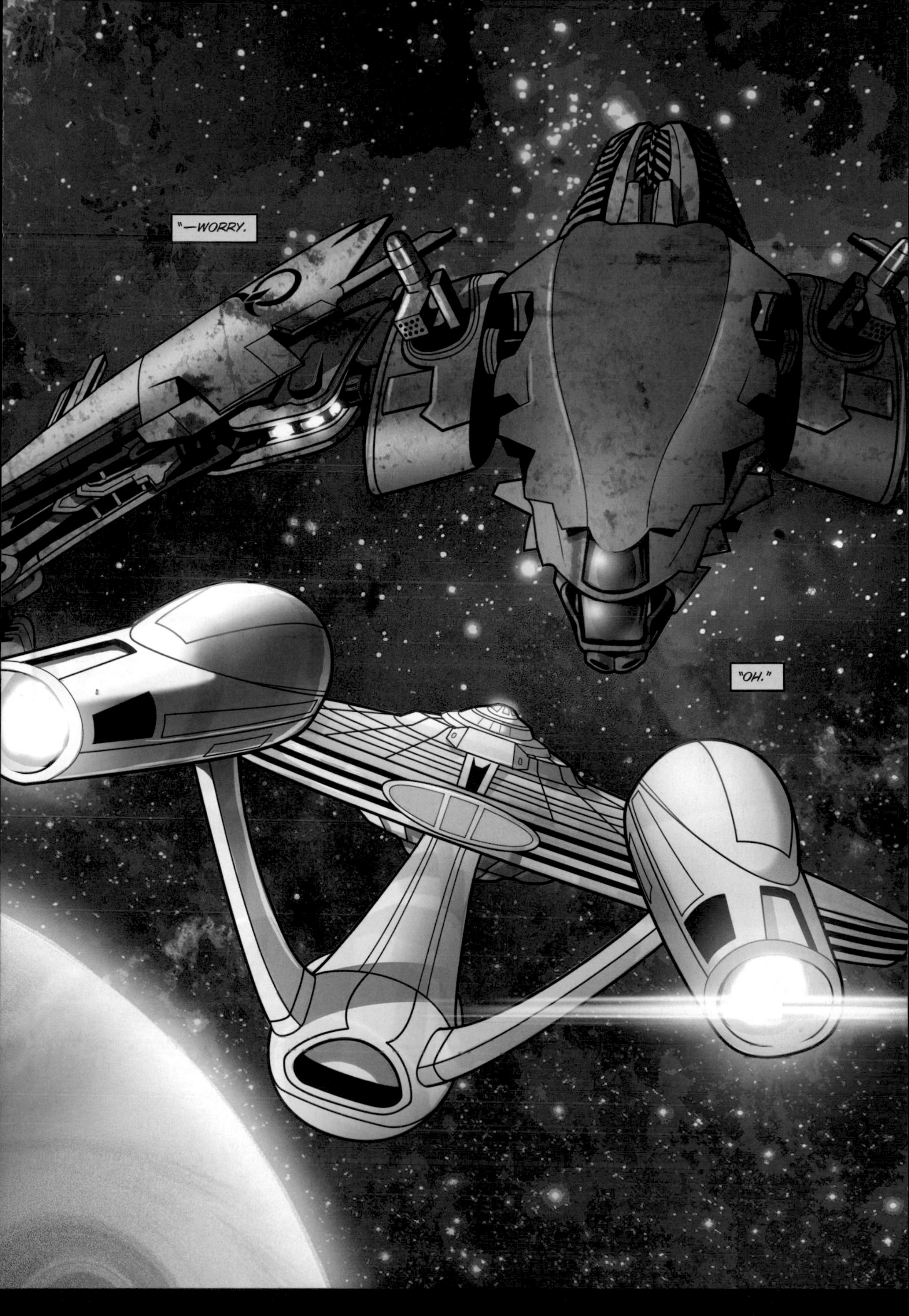
"—WORRY.
"OH."

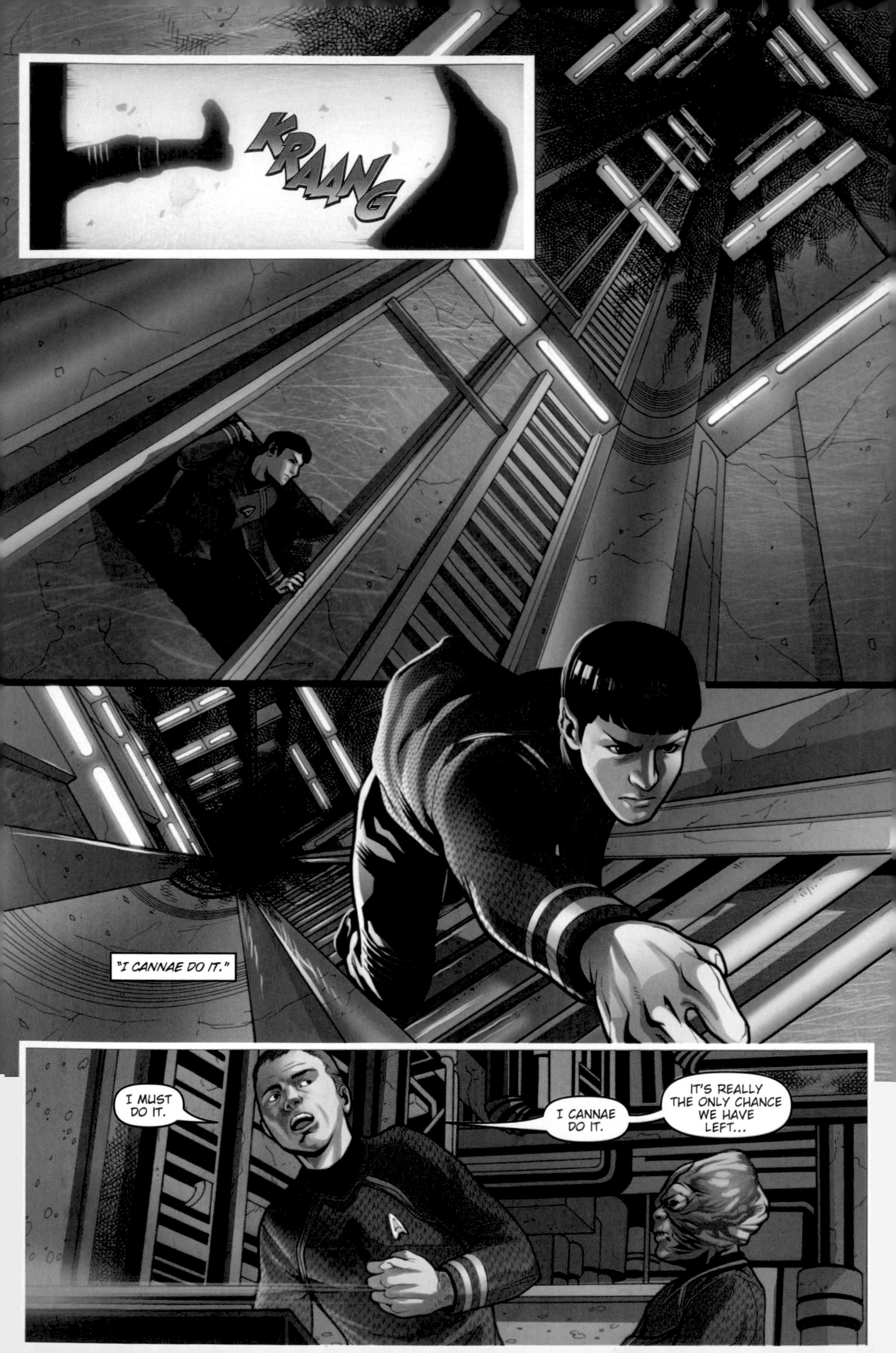
KRAANG
"I CANNAE DO IT."
I MUST DO IT.
I CANNAE DO IT.
IT'S REALLY THE ONLY CHANCE WE HAVE LEFT...

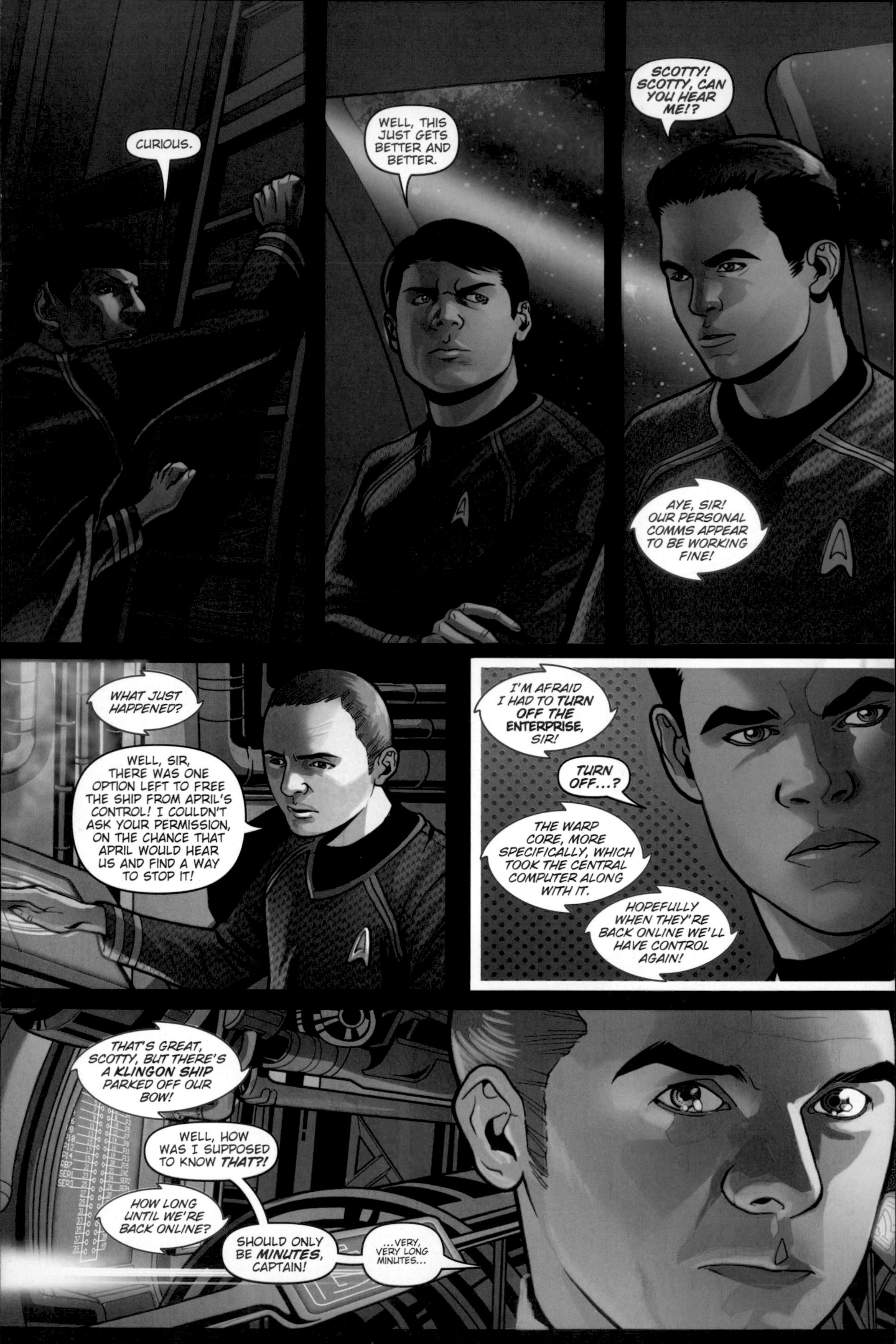
CURIOUS.
WELL, THIS JUST GETS BETTER AND BETTER.
SCOTTY! SCOTTY, CAN YOU HEAR ME!?
AYE, SIR! OUR PERSONAL COMMS APPEAR TO BE WORKING FINE!
WHAT JUST HAPPENED?
WELL, SIR, THERE WAS ONE OPTION LEFT TO FREE THE SHIP FROM APRIL'S CONTROL! I COULDN'T ASK YOUR PERMISSION, ON THE CHANCE THAT APRIL WOULD HEAR US AND FIND A WAY TO STOP IT!
I'M AFRAID I HAD TO TURN OFF THE ENTERPRISE, SIR!
TURN OFF...?
THE WARP CORE, MORE SPECIFICALLY, WHICH TOOK THE CENTRAL COMPUTER ALONG WITH IT.
HOPEFULLY WHEN THEY'RE BACK ONLINE WE'LL HAVE CONTROL AGAIN!
THAT'S GREAT, SCOTTY, BUT THERE'S A KLINGON SHIP PARKED OFF OUR BOW!
WELL, HOW WAS I SUPPOSED TO KNOW THAT?!
HOW LONG UNTIL WE'RE BACK ONLINE?
SHOULD ONLY BE MINUTES, CAPTAIN!
...VERY, VERY LONG MINUTES...

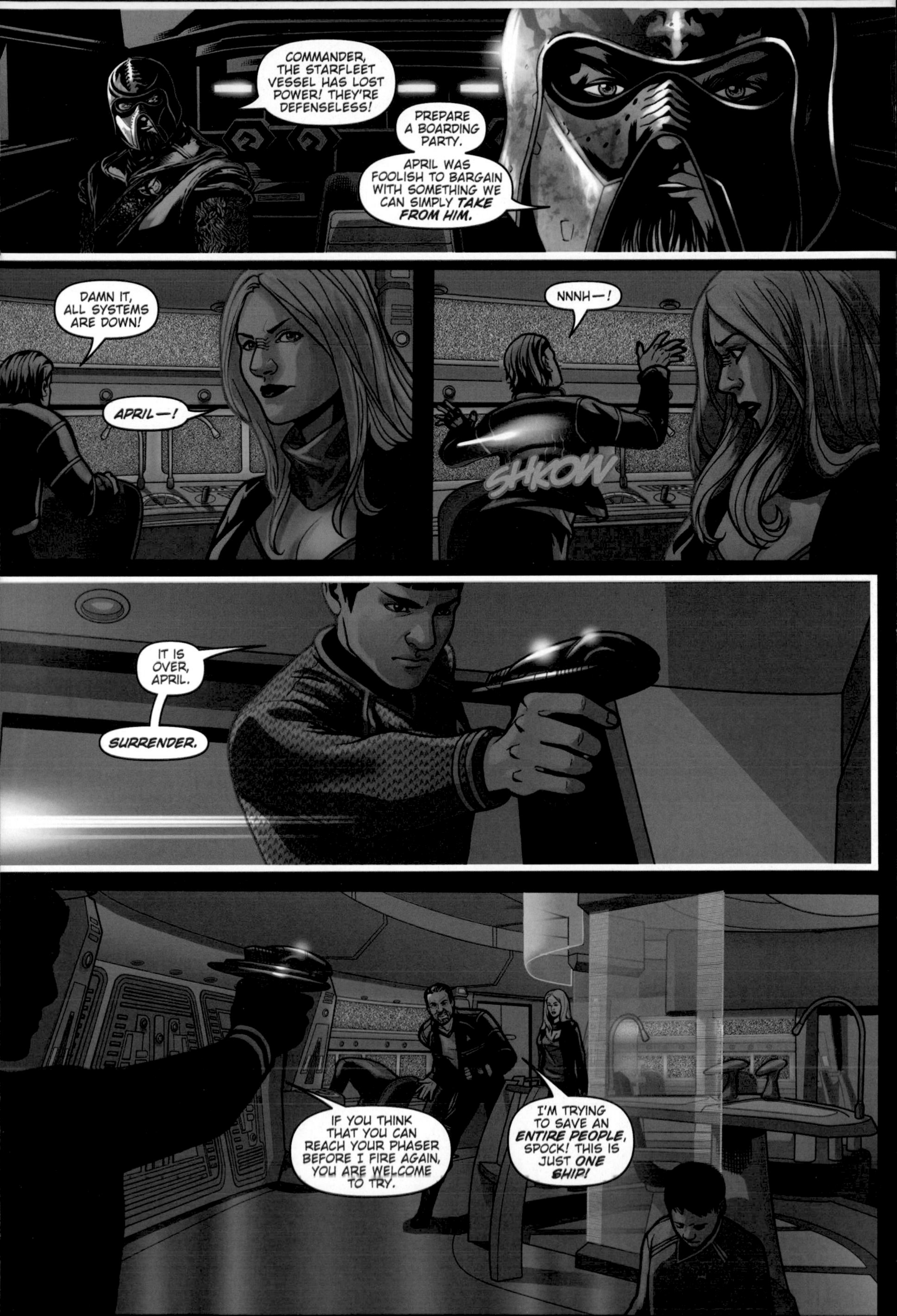
COMMANDER, THE STARFLEET VESSEL HAS LOST POWER! THEY'RE DEFENSELESS!
PREPARE A BOARDING PARTY.
APRIL WAS FOOLISH TO BARGAIN WITH SOMETHING WE CAN SIMPLY TAKE FROM HIM.
DAMN IT, ALL SYSTEMS ARE DOWN!
APRIL—!
NNNH—!
SHKOW
IT IS OVER, APRIL.
SURRENDER.
I'M TRYING TO SAVE AN ENTIRE PEOPLE, SPOCK! THIS IS JUST ONE SHIP!
IF YOU THINK THAT YOU CAN REACH YOUR PHASER BEFORE I FIRE AGAIN, YOU ARE WELCOME TO TRY.

"WHAT WERE YOU THINKING, APRIL?"

WERE YOU REALLY GOING TO JUST HAND OVER THE *ENTERPRISE* TO THE KLINGONS? MAKE ALL OF US PRISONERS OF THE EMPIRE, OR *WORSE*?

IF YOU DON'T UNDERSTAND BY NOW, KIRK, YOU NEVER WILL.

UNDERSTAND *WHAT*? YOU THINK THE KLINGONS WOULD HAVE LET YOU RULE PHAEDUS LIKE YOUR OWN PERSONAL KINGDOM?

YOU HONESTLY THINK YOU COULD SAVE YOUR FRIENDS THAT WAY?

YOU ALMOST STARTED A *WAR* THAT COULD KILL *BILLIONS* OF INNOCENTS!

IT'S QUAINT THAT YOU STILL THINK THIS WAR CAN BE *AVOIDED*, CAPTAIN.

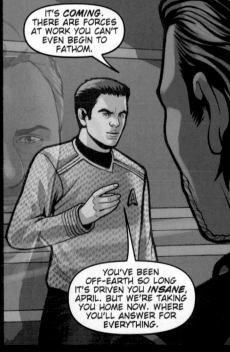

IT'S *COMING*. THERE ARE FORCES AT WORK YOU CAN'T EVEN BEGIN TO FATHOM.

YOU'VE BEEN OFF-EARTH SO LONG IT'S DRIVEN YOU *INSANE*, APRIL. BUT WE'RE TAKING YOU HOME NOW. WHERE YOU'LL ANSWER FOR EVERYTHING.

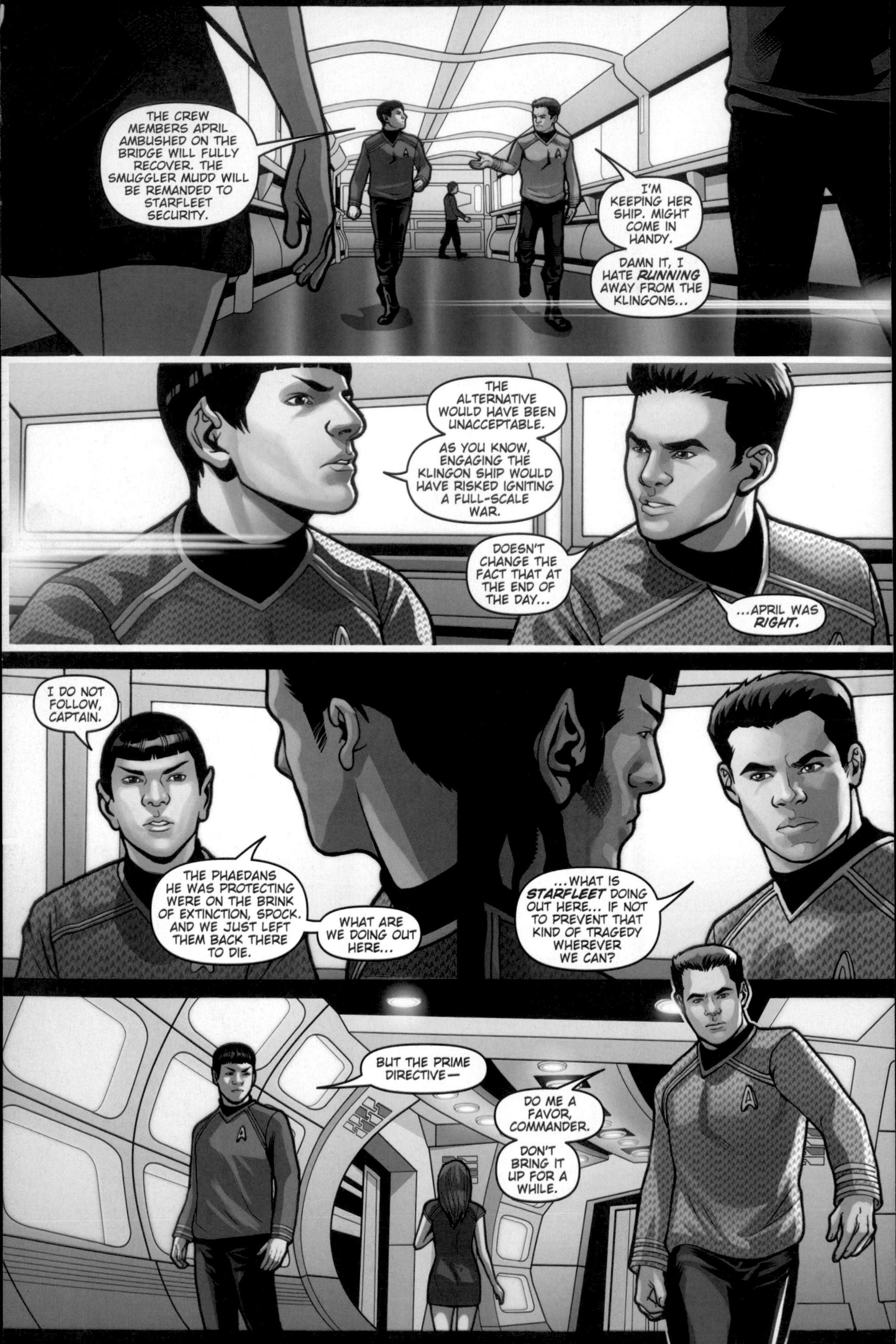
THE CREW MEMBERS APRIL AMBUSHED ON THE BRIDGE WILL FULLY RECOVER. THE SMUGGLER MUDD WILL BE REMANDED TO STARFLEET SECURITY.
I'M KEEPING HER SHIP. MIGHT COME IN HANDY.
DAMN IT, I HATE RUNNING AWAY FROM THE KLINGONS...
THE ALTERNATIVE WOULD HAVE BEEN UNACCEPTABLE.
AS YOU KNOW, ENGAGING THE KLINGON SHIP WOULD HAVE RISKED IGNITING A FULL-SCALE WAR.
DOESN'T CHANGE THE FACT THAT AT THE END OF THE DAY...
...APRIL WAS RIGHT.
I DO NOT FOLLOW, CAPTAIN.
THE PHAEDANS HE WAS PROTECTING WERE ON THE BRINK OF EXTINCTION, SPOCK. AND WE JUST LEFT THEM BACK THERE TO DIE.
WHAT ARE WE DOING OUT HERE...
...WHAT IS STARFLEET DOING OUT HERE... IF NOT TO PREVENT THAT KIND OF TRAGEDY WHEREVER WE CAN?
BUT THE PRIME DIRECTIVE—
DO ME A FAVOR, COMMANDER.
DON'T BRING IT UP FOR A WHILE.

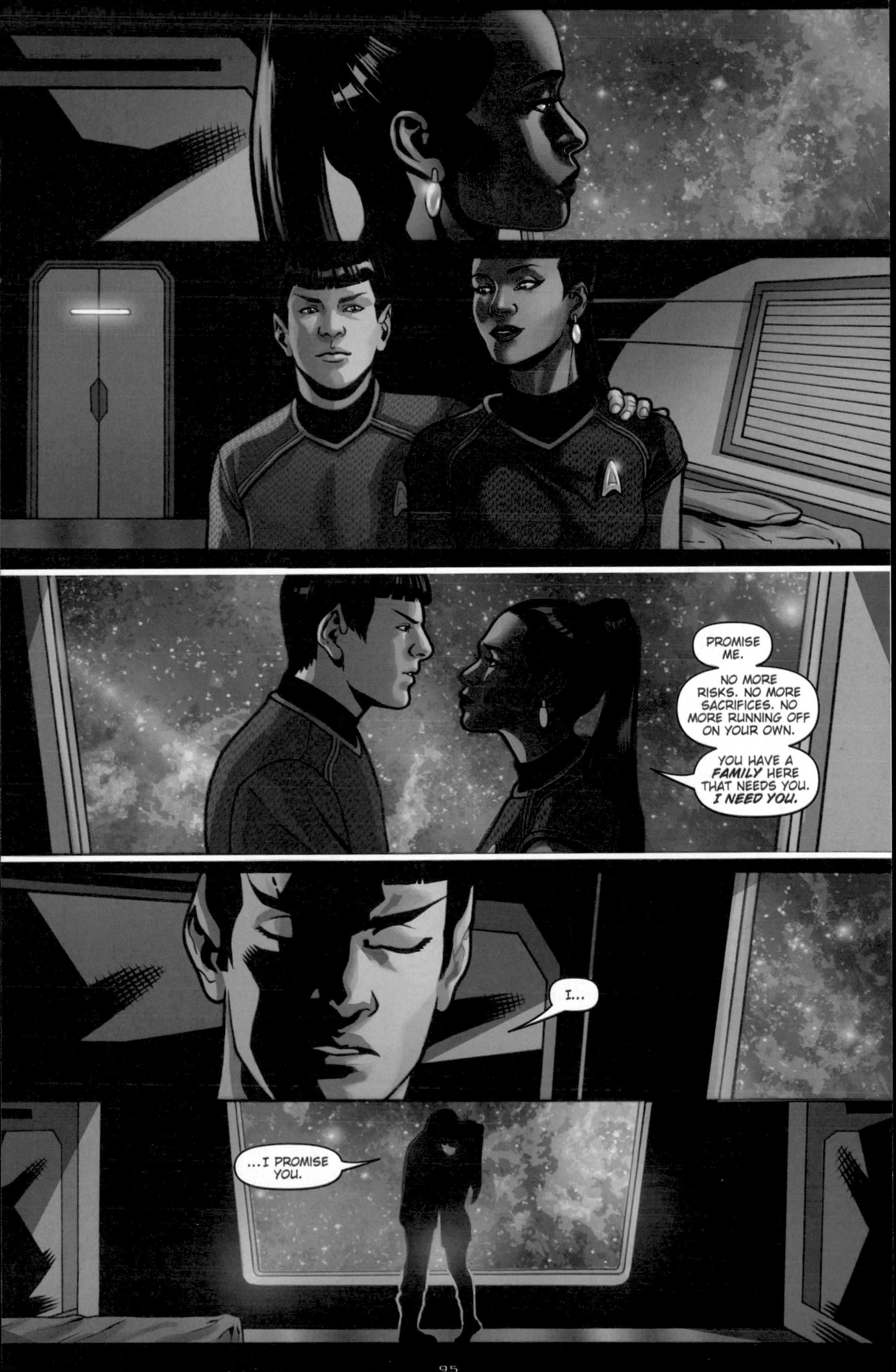
PROMISE ME.
NO MORE RISKS. NO MORE SACRIFICES. NO MORE RUNNING OFF ON YOUR OWN.
YOU HAVE A ***FAMILY*** HERE THAT NEEDS YOU. ***I NEED YOU.***
I...
...I PROMISE YOU.

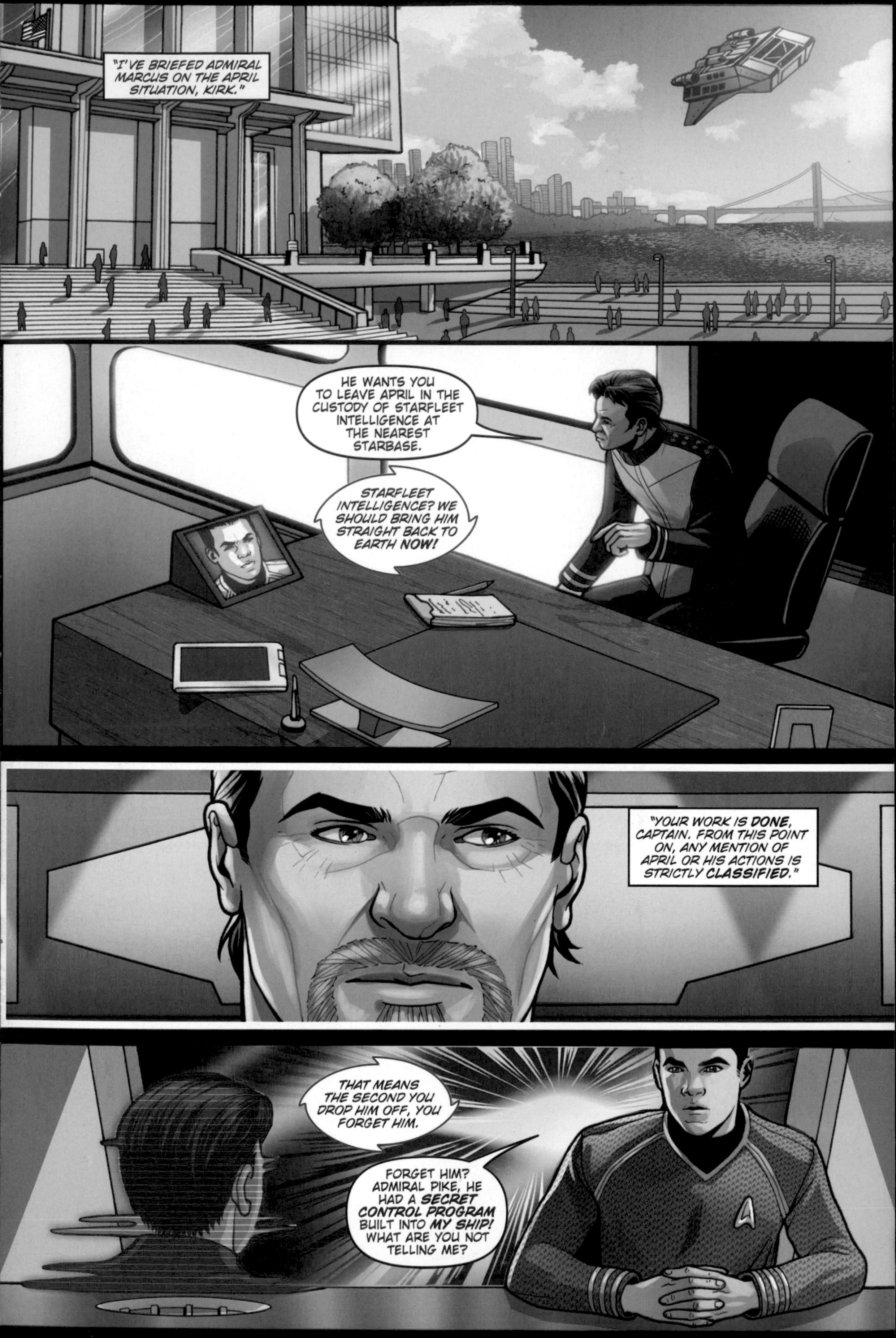
"I'VE BRIEFED ADMIRAL MARCUS ON THE APRIL SITUATION, KIRK."
HE WANTS YOU TO LEAVE APRIL IN THE CUSTODY OF STARFLEET INTELLIGENCE AT THE NEAREST STARBASE.
STARFLEET INTELLIGENCE? WE SHOULD BRING HIM STRAIGHT BACK TO EARTH NOW!
"YOUR WORK IS DONE, CAPTAIN. FROM THIS POINT ON, ANY MENTION OF APRIL OR HIS ACTIONS IS STRICTLY CLASSIFIED."
THAT MEANS THE SECOND YOU DROP HIM OFF, YOU FORGET HIM.
FORGET HIM? ADMIRAL PIKE, HE HAD A SECRET CONTROL PROGRAM BUILT INTO MY SHIP! WHAT ARE YOU NOT TELLING ME?

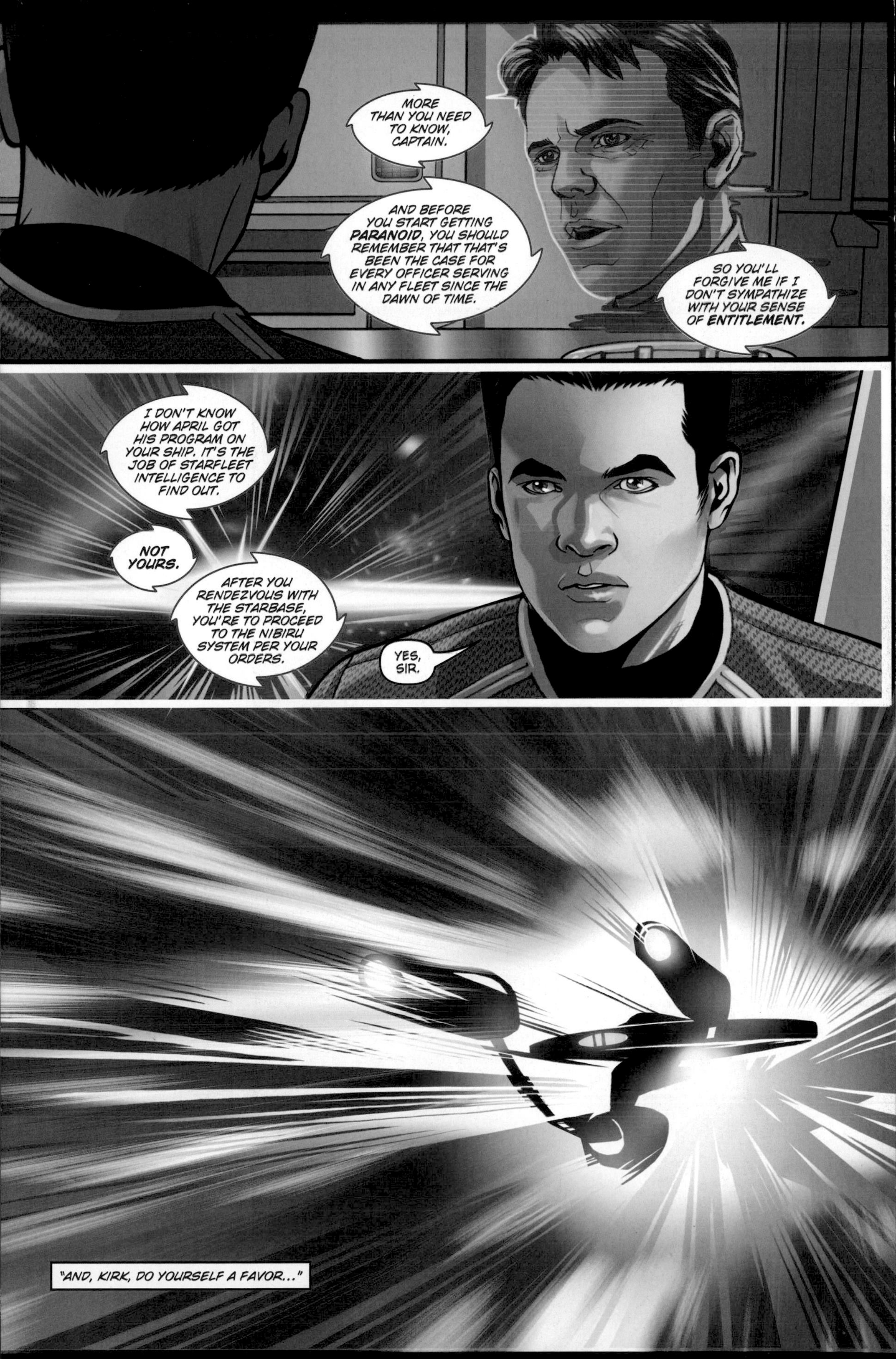
MORE THAN YOU NEED TO KNOW, CAPTAIN.
AND BEFORE YOU START GETTING **PARANOID**, YOU SHOULD REMEMBER THAT THAT'S BEEN THE CASE FOR EVERY OFFICER SERVING IN ANY FLEET SINCE THE DAWN OF TIME.
SO YOU'LL FORGIVE ME IF I DON'T SYMPATHIZE WITH YOUR SENSE OF **ENTITLEMENT**.
I DON'T KNOW HOW APRIL GOT HIS PROGRAM ON YOUR SHIP. IT'S THE JOB OF STARFLEET INTELLIGENCE TO FIND OUT.
NOT YOURS.
AFTER YOU RENDEZVOUS WITH THE STARBASE, YOU'RE TO PROCEED TO THE NIBIRU SYSTEM PER YOUR ORDERS.
YES, SIR.
"AND, KIRK, DO YOURSELF A FAVOR..."

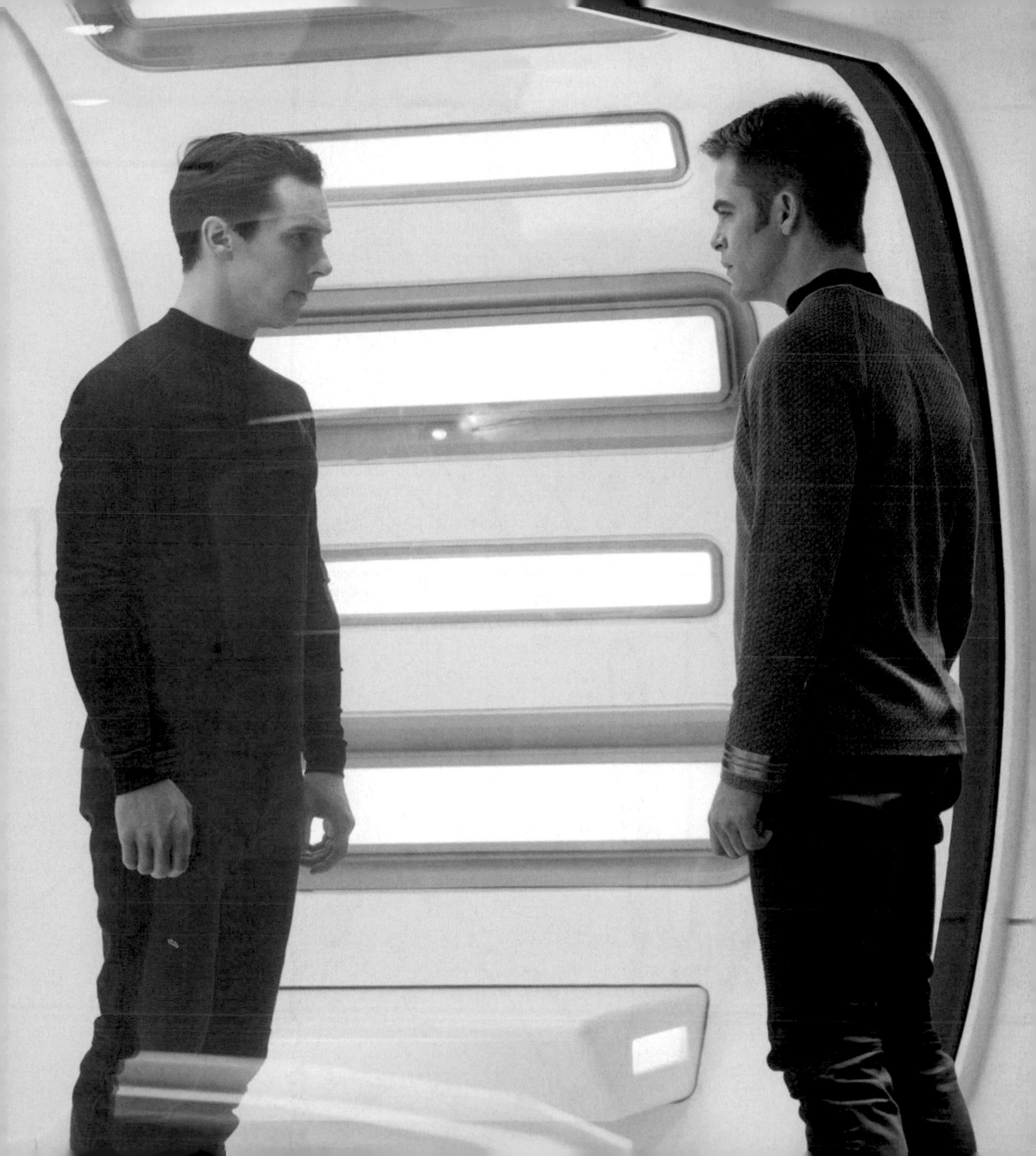

MESS -13

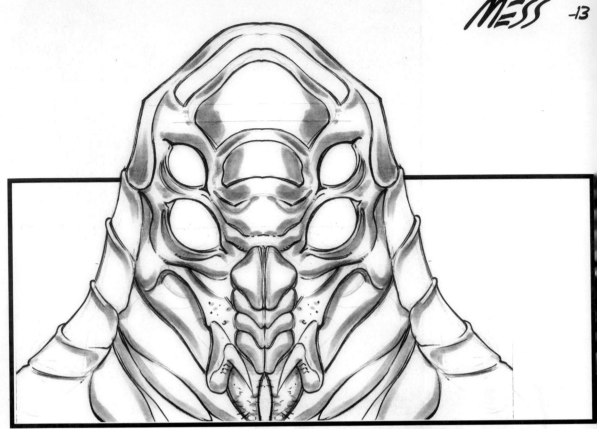

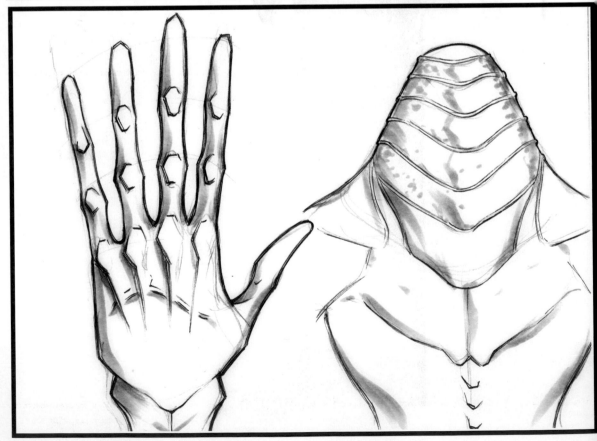

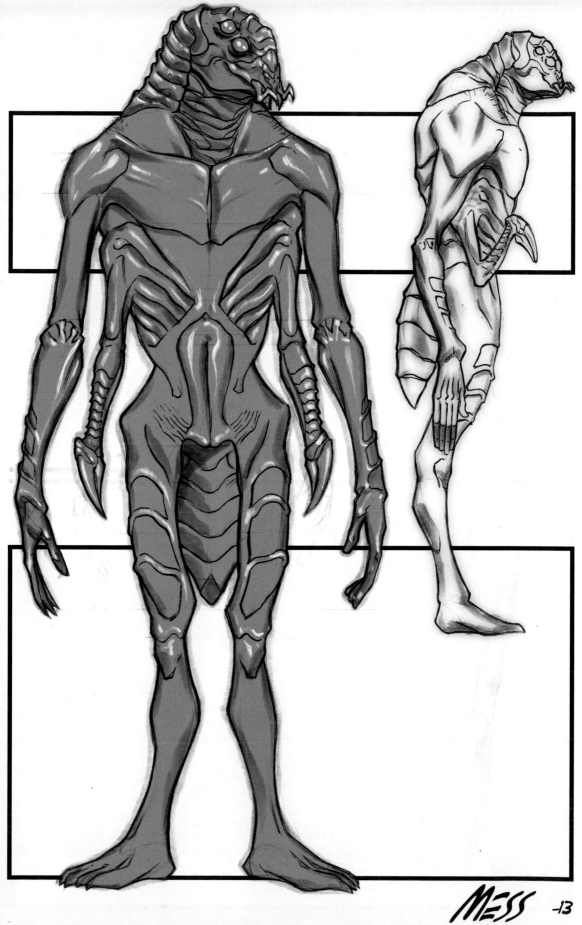

MESS -13

3D models by LINO GRANDI

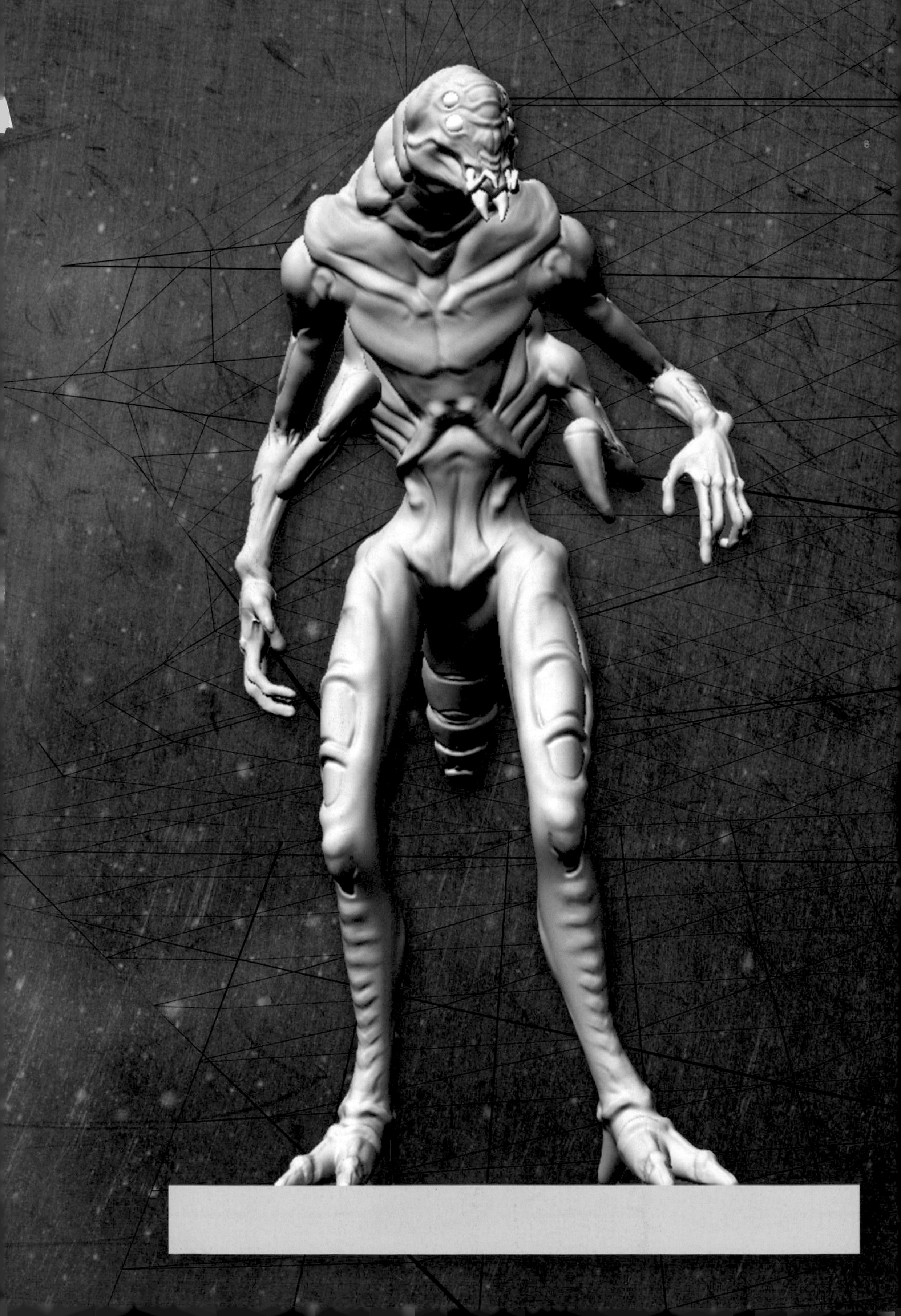

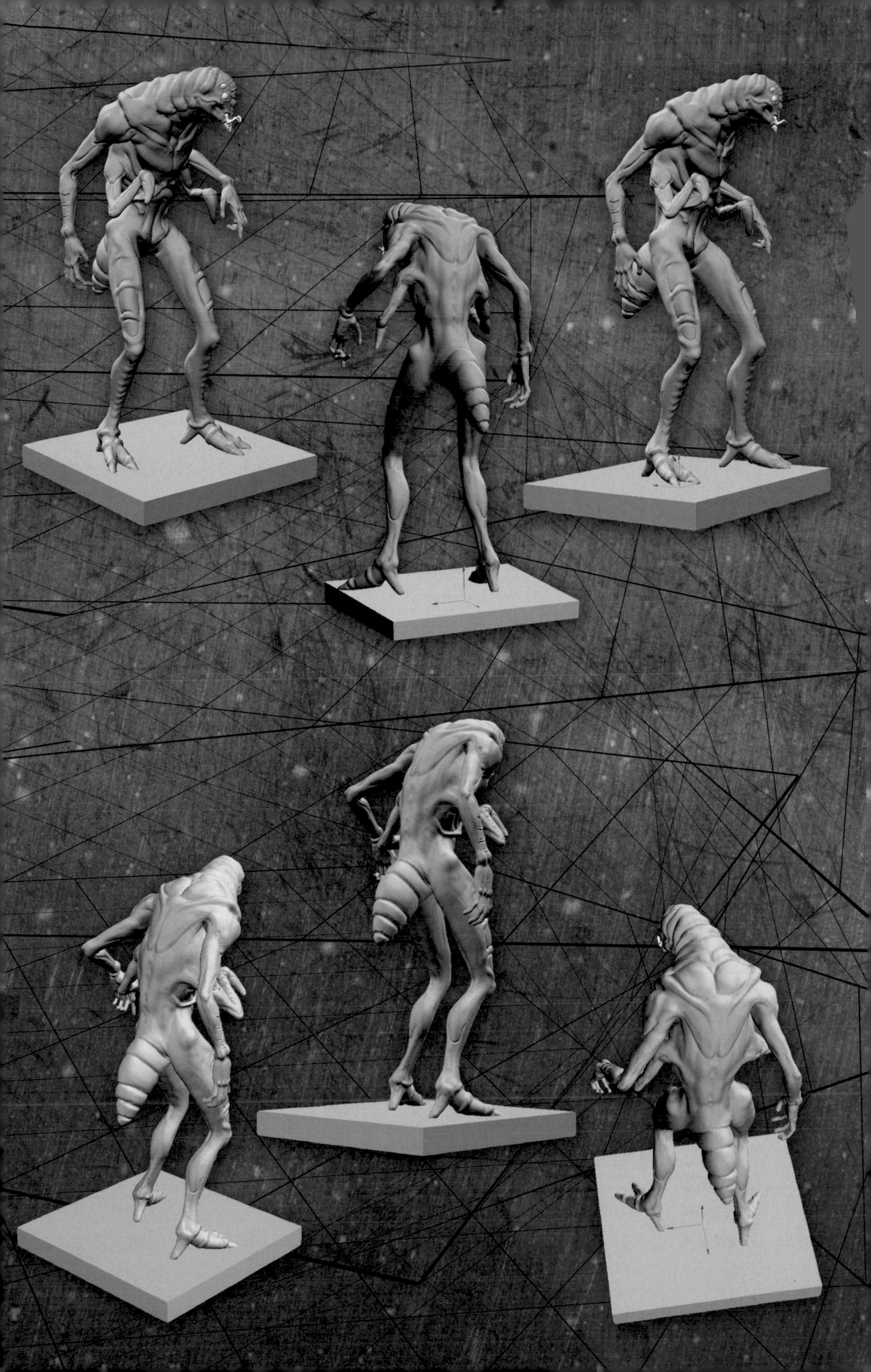

AFTERWORD

Movies are the **best**.

There's nothing better than settling into your seat in front of the biggest screen imaginable and being transported into an adventure that blows your mind. Thanks to amazing advances in visual effects, anything a filmmaker dreams up can be brought to cinematic life.

On behalf of the COUNTDOWN team, we hope this story whets your appetite for STAR TREK INTO DARKNESS. We feel grateful to work on Gene Roddenberry's epic creation in any capacity, and we hope our love for the characters comes through on every page.

Comics have a unique ability to portray both the grand scope of the STAR TREK universe and the more personal moments that are a hallmark of the series, without the need to pack it all into two hours.

Making comics means that we don't have to deal with the constraints of a movie's schedule and budget, or the pressure of launching a worldwide marketing campaign, or the headaches of dealing with everything that can go wrong at any moment on a massive soundstage. Making comics is the most direct way to get from the spark of an idea to a finished product that fans can enjoy.

Come to think of it…

Comics are the **best**.

Mike Johnson